# UNDERST/ DIMENSIONS AND TOLERANCES

## Geoffrey T. Johnson

C. Eng., M. I. Prod. E. (ret'd.)

Retired Industrial Designer and Senior Technical Manager.

Now part-time Engineering Lecturer.

Co-founder of the Halton Miniature Railway Society, Runcorn.

# DEDICATION

Ronnie Leatherbarrow, who taught me tool making as an apprentice, and Hans Gunter Otto Hirth, who taught me Dimensions and Tolerances as a new Designer.

Cover photograph of Southport College workshop, and

cover design by the author.

# CONTENTS

# PREFACE

It is an unfortunate fact that 95% of engineering designers do not appear to understand the basic principles of dimensioning or the effect of tolerances, and this lack of knowledge extends to the workshop, where many otherwise trained and experienced engineers have a similar lack of knowledge on the subject.

The problem is that the subject of dimensions and tolerances is not taught in Universities, Technical Colleges, or Workshop Technology books and even when it is, the teaching is done badly as the teachers are themselves in ignorance of the subject. It is a strange situation considering that dimensions and tolerances are the main aspects of engineering. This work is an attempt to lighten the darkness and help designers and engineers to improve their standards.

As far as aspiring designers and other engineering students are concerned, the BTec National course is an excellent foundation for building a future career in Engineering, but it is only the first few steps along a long road to mastering this technical subject.

Much has still to be learned in theory and practice. Although the emphasis in BTec courses is on developing practical skills, there will come a time when the theory has to be confronted and this usually happens when the student given the task of drawing an object.

**This book does not cover any specific assessment for any level, but is applicable to all drawing work which will be assessed.**

It sets out a list of good and bad practices and shows how designs, of even the simplest components, can be protected against workshop errors by thinking ahead. It is to be used alongside existing Workshop Drawing books, whose exercises should be completed.

What it aims to do is to show how to avoid repeating the bad practices and poor presentations of some of the examples in those drawing books.

Geoffrey T. Johnson, Runcorn. October 2016.

# CHAPTER 1.

## THE SCIENCE AND ART OF DIMENSIONING.

Before the advent of the modern computer, drawings were done with a pencil on drafting film fastened to a drawing board, but nowadays the vast majority of drawings are done on a PC through Computer Aided Design (CAD). The most widely used program of this type is 'AutoCAD' with its very capable 3D engine, and part of the course is learning how to use it.

In doing so it will be natural to think that 3D is always used for drawings, but this is a fallacy. In industry the vast majority of technical drawings only need flat plane, or orthographic, projections which are typically plan, side elevation, and end elevation, and for these the use of the 3D engine is unnecessary.

The 3D design engine has a major place in publishing where it is used for illustrations used in instruction sheets and maintenance manuals and is therefore of major interest to those wishing to become technical illustrators, but it has increasing use in 3D printing where a solid component can be directly made from a suitable image.

The problem with CAD is that the drawings it produces are usually of poor quality from both the program itself, especially early versions, and the program users. There are, regretfully, teachers of CAD who are theoretically trained but have no workshop experience, or have practical experience but no theoretical training. In both cases it is quite normal for them to have no drawing office experience at all, and their ignorance of dimensioning and presentation will be obvious.

It is not difficult to find examples of their work. When on line, simply ask the browser's search engine to find images of 'dimensioned technical drawings' and several hundred will appear. Clicking on the first and stepping through the examples may produce one similar to that shown in Fig.1.

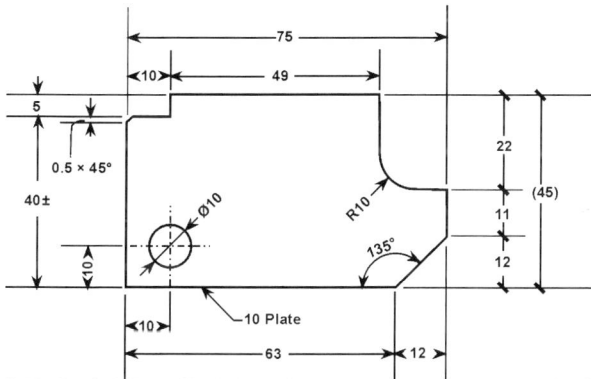

**Fig.1. A typical internet technical drawing.**

Superficially this drawing looks satisfactory, but it actually contains a lot of bad practices. Regretfully it is not unique, as 95% of all the images on the internet will be to the same poor standard. This appears to be the situation throughout industry which seems to think that this poor standard is the norm, when it should not be.

This dismal state of affairs can only have come about because dimensions and tolerances are:

- Seldom taught properly, if at all.
- Seldom discussed in technical drawing books, and even when they are the information is usually incorrect.

Associated with dimensions are tolerances, and these are:

- Generally understood singly, but not their overall effect.
- Seldom considered in 'Worst Case Scenarios', when all dimensions are worked to their maximum adverse tolerances.

Both of these shortcomings may be the cause of the poor level of skill which **can be seen** in the vast majority of drawings, but note the words *'can be seen'*. A trained engineer can tell at a glance whether the person who created the drawing:

- Understood dimensioning.
- Understood tolerances.
- Understood presentation.
- Used bad practices.
- Had practical experience.
- Knew Drawing Office practice.

So the drawing will not only show whether that person is competent or incompetent but it will also identify that person by the initials or name they put in the 'Drawn by' box.

Incompetence is revealed in bad practices, poor dimensioning, and inferior presentation. Even the workshop drawing manuals used in, and drawings supplied to, Technical Colleges can contain illustrations which exhibit any or all of these faults, even though they were drawn by people employed for such work. It is well to remember that:

**"The drawing will reveal your competence or otherwise."**

Technical drawing is both a science and an art. The science requires a through knowledge of Arithmetic, Geometry, and Trigonometry, as all are used in the of drawings, so these subjects must be learned and applied. Mental arithmetic is of especial value, and the more it can be practiced, the better. Workshop Technology is equally important as the drawing's creator has to know the capabilities of the workshop in which the drawing will become a reality - what is possible and what is not. For example, it is no use calling for a surface to be ground flat if there is no surface grinder available.

## THE SCIENCE OF DRAWING.

The science involves:

- Practical knowledge. A grounding in workshop practice is highly desirable.
- Theoretical knowledge. This includes arithmetic, geometry, and trigonometry, and these mathematic subjects will need to

be mastered. Further education will be also needed to study other subjects, such as materials and heat treatment.

- Understanding dimensions and tolerances, the subject of this book.
- Adherence to the tenets of the current Drawing Office standard (BS8888), so that drawings will follow its methodology.

## THE ART OF PRESENTATION.

The art involves:

- Personal experience of drawing and design. It is of great benefit if the person who designs an item can actually make it.
- Presentational style. This develops with experience, but studying bad and good examples will help at the start.
- Clarity and legibility. This is very important in order to avoid wrong interpretations by workshop personnel.

Inevitably for a subject which can be an art as well as a science, there are some examples of bad design caused by incorrect principles being applied, and others due to a lack of theoretical knowledge or practical skills.

Occasionally someone who has had no workshop experience will create a drawing with a component which is either impossible to make or prove very expensive to manufacture. Errors of this kind are usually detected by the Office Checker, but now and again one will slip through the net.

A simple example of a bad design is an component drawn by someone with technical but no practical knowledge. It looked perfectly feasible when drawn but fortunately it was rejected by the Checker. This is shown in Fig.2.

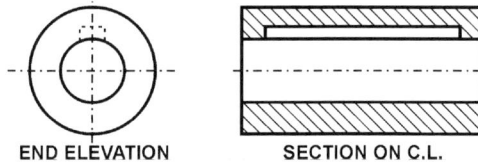

END ELEVATION        SECTION ON C.L.

**Fig.2. Collar with a blind keyway.**

The section shows a keyway in the bore, but it does not run right through the length of the collar. This is referred to as a 'blind' keyway, and it is impossible to machine in small bore sizes. Even in large sizes, i.e. more than 300 mm diameter, it would require special equipment to do it. It is far easier to cut the slot right through, as shown in Fig.3, which is a practical design.

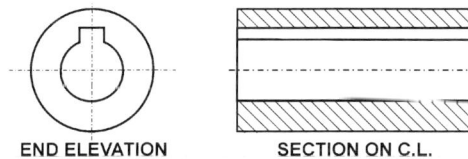

END ELEVATION        SECTION ON C.L.

**Fig.3. Collar with a through keyway.**

## BAD DESIGN.

One of the worst examples of bad design, due to the theoretical-but-no-practical knowledge of its perpetrator, occurred in an reputable engine works in the 1950's. It was issued, since it was not realised during the examination of the drawing in the Drawing Office that it was badly designed.

It was a cast iron hollow box almost a cube around 300mm (12"), as shown in Fig.4, and it was nicknamed "The Biscuit Tin" by the shop floor staff, as biscuits were often packed in tins of that size.

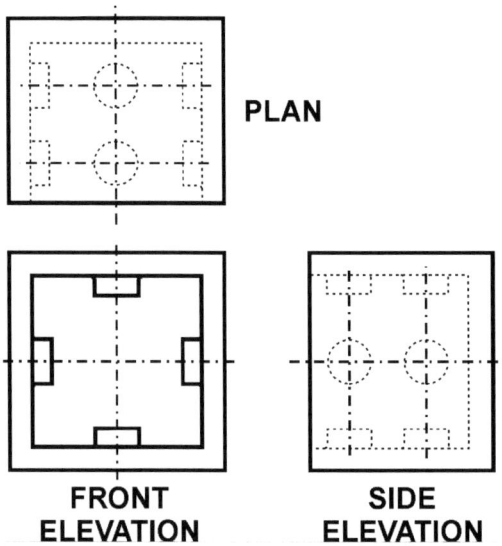

PLAN

FRONT
ELEVATION

SIDE
ELEVATION

**Fig.4. "The Biscuit Tin".**

The components were to be machined on several manually-operated Horizontal Borers, which are milling machines similar to a lathe but with a rise-and-fall headstock and tailstock. Inside the Biscuit Tin there were eight internal pads, two per side. These had to be machined so that a square block would slide inside the box. A schematic diagram of the set-up is shown in Fig.5.

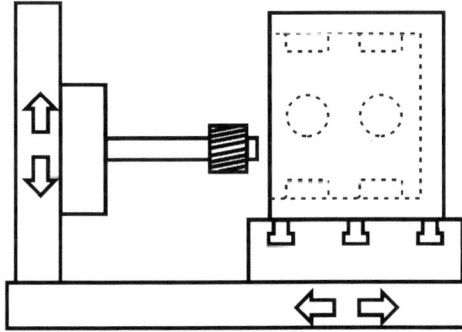

**Fig.5. "The Biscuit Tin" mounted on the Boring Table.**

The machine's cross slide, headstock, and carriage motions would allow all the bosses to be machined, but when the carriage had moved the component towards the headstock so the inner pads could be machined, the situation appeared as in Fig.6.

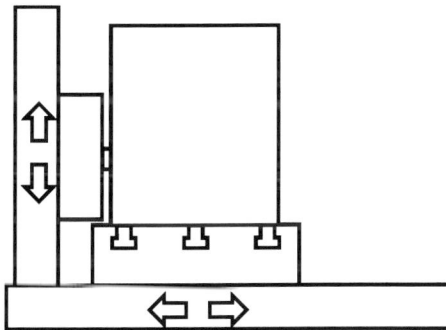

**Fig.6. The situation when machining the inner pads.**

In this situation the operators could not see the cutter or the pads so had no visual feedback and had to work by sound, which is not easy to do in a noisy engine works. As a result the machinists scrapped 95% of the parts despite their skills. Although the scrapped parts could be reclaimed by welding, the cost of all the hours of unnecessary work can only be guessed.

It was only then seen to have been a bad design because the capability of the workshop to do the job had not been taken into account. Clearly its perpetrator was not versed in the manual operation of the machines. It really needed a total redesign, but even with the existing design the machinist's task could have made easier if a little bit of practical knowledge had been applied, as shown in Fig.7.

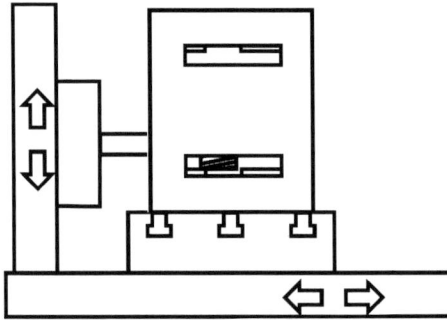

**Fig.7. "The Biscuit Tin" with viewing slots.**

One aspect of creating a drawing which is often overlooked, and was overlooked in this example, is that every component will have a minimum cost to produce it, i.e. material and machining time and overhead costs, etc., as shown on an estimate before the profit margin is added. It is the draughtsman or CAD operator's job to ensure that it can be made to that cost.

Whatever its form it has to be within the capability of the workshop. The extent of the workshop facilities, and that of subcontractors, needs to be understood. The example of the Biscuit Tin already discussed shows how important this knowledge is to good drawing work. If the method of machining it is not known at the time the drawing is produced, then it should be investigated before starting. It is probably best to discuss with the workshop staff a draft drawing of the projected component, and follow their recommendations before finalising the drawing.

## THE OBJECT IN CREATING A DRAWING.

The object is to ensure that the component can be produced in a cost effective way, but no matter how well designed any component may be, the result will not the one intended if the workshop does not do its job properly, so the drawing has to be clear and unambiguous.

In the Drawing Office the rule is that 'the buck stops here', therefore its personnel should try to ensure that errors in component manufacture are not attributed to them. The way the component is to be made should be reflected in the way that it is dimensioned, so that adherence to the dimensions will produce an acceptable result. This means understanding the thinking behind the dimensioning.

If a component, especially a complex one, fails inspection due to faulty workmanship it is not uncommon for the workshop to blame the drawing. In answer to that it should always be possible for the drawing's creator to say, **"It's not the drawing's fault because the dimensions were not followed."** That means the method of dimensioning needs to be thoroughly understood. It is in the designer's own interest to anticipate possible disaster points and try to mitigate them at the outset. Some ways of doing this will be given later.

# CHAPTER 2.

## DIMENSIONING TECHNIQUES.

There is no such a thing as a 'standard' drawing, since every object has different requirements and needs to be handled as an individual component or assembly. Therefore judgement is involved and as a result hard-and-fast rules cannot be laid down. Instead guidance on how to dimension and present a drawing will be given by comparing bad and good examples. In any case experience is the best master, as the difference between a beginner and an expert is how many hours the expert has put into his craft.

Examples of poor presentation abound, even in technical textbooks and workshop drawing manuals. In due course reproductions of some published examples which were professionally-drawn will be given, although none will pinpoint the source. There will also be examples of bad or non-preferred practices and, as good drawing practice is the object here, alternative versions will be offered to show how to avoid them. It must also be borne in mind that some technical drawings come from other countries and may include different standards and conventions which do not match, or may even conflict with, those used in the home country.

Many people seem to throw dimensions at a drawing more in hope than expectation, but it is one thing to dimension a drawing and another to anticipate what the result will be of making it to those dimensions. Bad dimensioning leads to increased cost and waste of materials, whilst poor presentation makes a drawing hard to read and so causes misinterpretations to be made. **Dimensions should be applied to those aspects needing control, not to ones which are unimportant**, but this will be discussed in detail later.

## DRAWING SHEETS.

Every drawing requires a sheet upon which it is drawn, whether it is on a drawing board or a CAD station. This sheet will have a frame near the edge, an information panel which is a section at the bottom of the sheet containing general information, and a space for the drawing itself. The section at the bottom can be laid out in several ways, but is usually standardised in a company.

The panel will contain a number of boxes to be completed, and are usually for the following information:

- Drawing Number.
- Drawn by.
- Date.
- Scale.
- Tolerance.
- Material used.

- Issue letter or number and date.
- Name of the organisation or office.

There is no set arrangement for these boxes, but it is common for the drawing number to be on the extreme right, and the organisation's name on the extreme left. All these boxes will need completion before the drawing is issued.

In the area reserved for the drawing there will be other information around the edges. These concern the projection system (First or Third Angle) used in the drawing and whether the drawing is imperial, using feet and inches, or metric, using metres and millimetres. Engineering does not normally use other multiples or sub-divisions, and feet and inches or millimetres are the norm in drawings.

## DATUMS.

Before commencing to draw any component it is important to know that all dimensions are taken from Datums (another plural form of the word 'Datum'. The alternative Latin plural 'Data', has a different meaning). Datums can be points, lines, edges, faces, or holes. Datum points are usually corners or the centres of circles, and a single datum point, which is usually the centre of a sphere or a corner, can be the origin of dimensions in all three planes. Datum Lines may be centre lines which straddle several components, e.g. crankshaft bearings.

The Datums required for the component to be drawn have to be decided at the outset. For details generally the most important aspects will be the edges, and three will be needed, one for each plane. Datum edges and faces are the normal origins for the dimensions, but what has to be borne in mind is that whilst one edge or face may be flat and accurate enough to act as a datum, another may be too rough for the purpose.

Typical examples are sawn bar stock and castings. In these cases a sawn edge, or the appropriate face of a casting, will require machining first. Where this is known the machining requirement is shown by an '$f$' mark (meaning 'finish machine'). This tells the constructor to make this edge flat and square to the other datums before doing anything else.

Normally this would mean machining the appropriate face which is usually performed on a milling machine, but in BTec practical fitting courses the datum is usually achieved by filing flat and square in both directions, as shown in Fig.8.

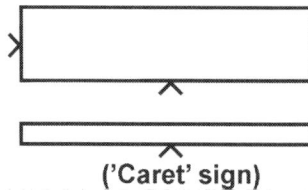
('Caret' sign)

**Fig.8. Choosing the Datums.**

Datum faces are indicated by a caret sign ('V' mark). The datums are usually at:

- One side, which is usually at the bottom.

- The left hand end.

- One face.

Occasionally it may be more convenient to use the right hand side as a datum, but this is uncommon and not preferred. The exception is for long work where datums are required at both ends, as on frame spacers.

A datum can be transferred to a hole from and edge, making it a Datum Hole, as shown in Fig.9.

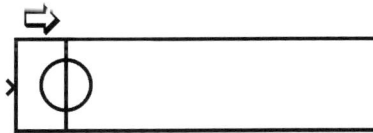

**Fig.9. Transferring a Datum to a Hole.**

The datum can also be transferred from the Datum Hole to the edge or another hole. A Datum Hole can be recognised from the fact that from the edge to the hole there will be only one dimension, whereas there could be several dimensions from the hole.

## DRAWING A COMPONENT.

When drawing a component it is necessary to consider how it is going to be made, since the draughtsman or CAD operator is 'virtually' making it on the drawing board or the monitor screen. There are several things to note about dimensioning:

- **Projection lines** are perpendicular to the face being measured.
- **Dimension lines are** parallel to the surface and end with arrowheads at the projection lines. They also have the dimensional figures above them. In the vertical plane the figure should read from the right.
- The **thickness** of the projection and dimension lines is approximately half of the component's outline thickness.
- No 'rugby goalposts'. The projection lines do not need to be more than 2 - 3mm beyond the dimension line.
- All dimensions start at the appropriate datum, as shown by the datum indicator (caret sign).
- The digits assigned to the dimension should be clearly written and properly formed if using a pencil. If using CAD then a good, clear font should be used, Arial being ideal. In A4 these should be 14pt or 3.5mm high. If the drawing is to be scaled down to A4 from A3 or larger then the original font size should be increased in direct ratio so that the finished drawing has the sizes stated. A3 → A4 use 20pt; A2 → A4 use 28pt; A1 → A4 use 40pt; A0 → A4 use 56pt.
- The triangular arrowheads should be well-formed and have a good proportion (e.g. 2.5 - 4 × width). The physical size will largely depend upon the size of the drawing sheet, A0 sizes usually having much larger arrowheads than those for A4, the

size being judged by the font size used. In Fig.10 are some examples of bad lines and arrowheads, and a good example.

**Fig.10. Bad and Good Arrowheads.**

In Fig.11 the component on the left is taken from an American CAD drawing published on the Internet. On the right is the same component as drawn by a pencil draughtsman.

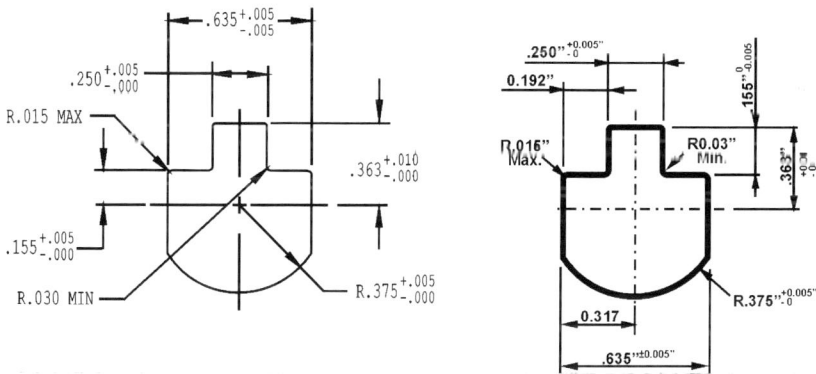

**Fig.11. Typical CAD and Pencil Drawings.**

Note that the pencil drawing has different line thicknesses for outline and dimensions, whereas the CAD drawing has no difference in the line width. In the pencil; drawing the measurements are from a centre line, and the top two dimensions are not related to the vertical centre line. The centre line, like the equator, is not a real line but a virtual one, and impossible to use as a basis for measurement.

One of the reasons why the use of CAD seems to have lowered

drawing standards is that most of the CAD drawings examined so far have had a uniform line thickness, width, or 'weight' throughout, whereas pencil draughtsmen used several widths. This is very common on CAD drawings, and the reason may be that CAD operators do not know how to change the line thickness.

How it is done in 'AutoCAD' is given below, but other CAD systems will use similar methods.

## ADJUSTING THE LINE THICKNESS IN 'AutoCAD'.

### Method A - Polylines (Shapes).

- From the DRAW Toolbar pick the Polyline icon.
- Click to define the start of the polyline.
- When prompted, insert the START WIDTH and ENTER.
- Repeat 3 with same figure for END WIDTH.
- After starting the line type 'W>' ENTER to change thickness.

### Method B - Lineweights (PaperSpace).

- From FORMAT Menu pick LAYERS.
- In LAYER MANAGER select desired LAYER.
- Select the LINEWEIGHT (Use a wide one for outlines).
- Close the LAYER MANAGER and commence drawing.
- Choose a new layer for the other details.

- Select a narrower LINEWEIGHT for it.

When the two widths are satisfactory, take note of both sizes and always use them.

**N.B. When scaling drawings up or down, ModelSpace gives constant line thickness and PaperSpace gives scale line thickness.**

## ADJUSTING THE THICKNESS OF PENCIL LINES.

This is done by the way the pencil is sharpened. The small pencil sharpener commonly used in schools and at home is taboo in a Drawing Office.

The reason is that it puts a rather short conical nose and point onto the pencil, as shown in Fig.12, and the point wears rapidly leading to a tapering line and inconsistency in the drawing.

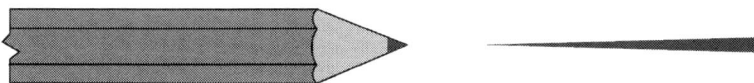

**Fig.12. Pencil Sharpened with a Pencil Sharpener.**

The method of sharpening Drawing Office pencils requires the use of the sharpener shown in Fig.13.

**Fig.13. Small Craft Knife.**

These can be purchased in a model or pound shop, and they have snap-off blades so blunt ends can be removed. When snapping off a worn end-section, make sure it is wrapped in adhesive tape to prevent it causing injury.

When travelling with such a knife make sure it is retracted and inside a container, not on the person, as it could be considered an offensive weapon. Normally the Drawing Office will have a larger version, but many draughtsmen like to keep a small one in their pencil box.

There are two stages in sharpening a Drawing Office pencil. The first stage is shown in Fig.14.

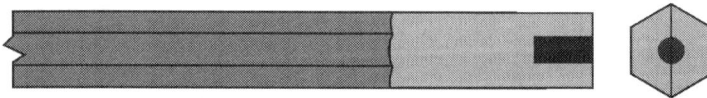

**Fig.14. First Stage in sharpening a Drawing Pencil.**

The end is cut into a long flat wedge shape, the lead being treated the same as the wood. This taper may be as much as 50% longer than that put on by the pencil sharpener above.

**Fig.15.  Second Stage in Sharpening a Drawing Pencil.**

The second stage is shown in Fig.15.The two sides are now tapered inwards to create a narrow chisel end, so the line width will vary according to which way around the pencil is held. The longer taper means that the thickness of the thinner line produced does not increase as much as with the conically-cut lead, and is maintained by the use of glass paper. This is obtainable from stationers in blocks with dimensions in the order of 75mm x 20mm. When dressing the end, using an axial movement means the wood will be removed as well as the lead to keep the taper constant. A Pencil Holder can be used when the pencil gets too short to hold.

## ADJUSTING MECHANICAL PENCIL LINE THICKNESS.

Mechanical pencils come in two varieties: Clutch, and Self-Propelling, and both use refillable leads, as shown in Fig.16.

**Fig.16. Clutch and Propelling Drawing Pencils.**

The propelling pencil (top) has a press button on the barrel to feed the refill lead and often has an eraser at the top which acts as a lid for a spare leads container inside. It is intended for one size of lead only, but the necessary clearance between the lead and its guide tube means that there is a little bit of play or 'wobble' at the writing tip, which can be a nuisance when drawing, but otherwise its press-button action makes maintaining the length of exposed lead easier.

The clutch pencil (bottom) has a chuck at the business end, and lead release is actuated by a push button at the other. The refill lead is held firmly near to the drawing surface. It will also hold spare leads inside the barrel, and it is capable of holding different sizes of lead so it is more versatile than the propelling pencil but control of lead length is manual.

Correct Drawing Office practice requires that two distinct line widths are used on technical drawings. See Fig.17 for line widths and their usages. These usages should not be confused.

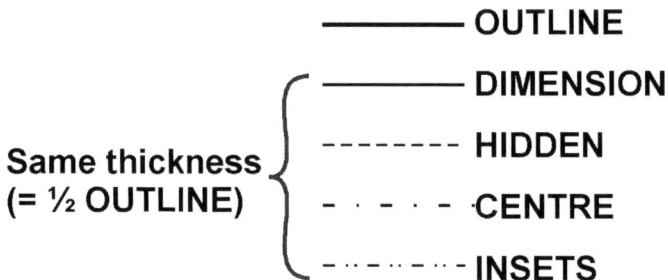

OUTLINE

DIMENSION

Same thickness
(= ½ OUTLINE)

HIDDEN

CENTRE

INSETS

**Fig.17. Various Lines and their Usages.**

The thicker line is for component outlines, and the other thinner lines for their own special purposes as shown. These lines should never be confused in their use. Two line widths are easy to obtain with a single wooden pencil, but the big advantage with mechanical pencils is that the line width stays constant. The easiest method of using mechanical pencils is to have two, one for each of the two diameters of lead, and are kept only for that purpose.

As far as dimensioning is concerned, many drawings show vertical dimensions with the figure upright but this is not considered good practice in the BSI standard. Splitting the dimension line and inserting the dimension, whether horizontal or vertical, is also not good practice. The dimension line should be continuous with the dimension above it and at right angles to the face being measured. Fig.18 shows both bad and good practice for vertical dimensions. Vertical dimensions should read from the right hand side.

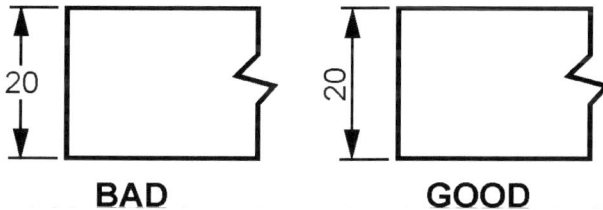

**Fig.18. Bad and Good Ways of Vertical Dimensioning.**

In Fig.19 basic dimensions have been added to the simple prepared Block shown earlier. Both dimensions are taken from their respective datum edges. The dimension, 'L', is placed alongside the length, and the dimension, 'W', placed alongside the width.

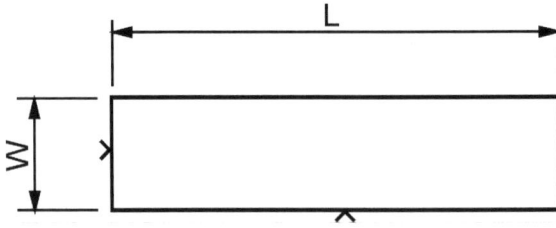

**Fig.19. Simple Block with Basic Dimensions.**

Figs. 8, 9, 18, and 19 were single views, but most drawings are generally done with three views: Plan, Side Elevation, and End Elevation, although on simple parts a Side or End Elevation may not be necessary, and a simple thickness dimension given instead. There may also be additional sectional views through various parts. The question then arises as to how to present these views.

- **Elevations** are external views of components or assemblies.

- **Sections** show internal details, and are often described as 'Section on …' with a pair of letters added. The letters appear at each end of a line which indicates where the section is to be taken, which is an imaginary cut through the part.

- When the view cuts through solid material the section is shown 'hatched', i.e. filled with parallel diagonal lines. To differentiate between different parts the pitch of the lines may vary and the angle of inclination fixed at either 45° or 135°. 'Scrap Views' are part-elevations to show aspects of complex drawings which need clarifying.

## PROJECTION METHODS.

Fig.20 shows one method of presenting three views of a stepped block. In this projection the End and Side Elevations are each placed on the opposite side of the Plan to the viewing position, and this method is called *First Angle Projection.*

This projection is normally not mentioned on drawings as it was the original method universally used until the start of the Second World War in 1939. With this projection the Plan is usually placed at the bottom.

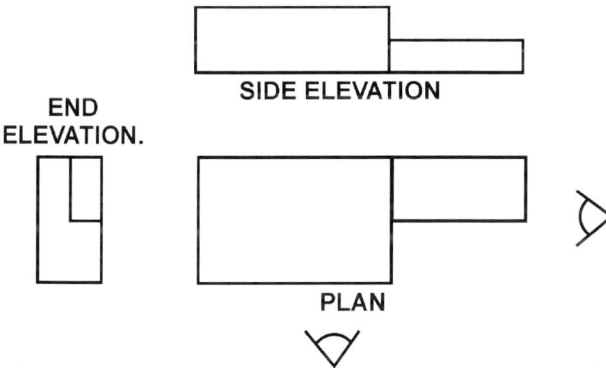

**Fig.20. First Angle Projection.**

In World War II the Americans brought with them drawings which had a different projection method which was called at the time, *'American Projection.*

In Fig.21 the End and Side Elevations are each placed on the same side of the Plan as the viewing position (i.e. between the Plan and the viewing position), and this method is now called *Third Angle*

*Projection.* In this system the Plan is usually at the top.

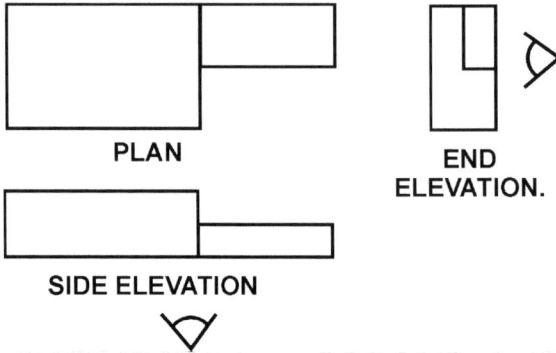

**Fig.21. Third Angle (or American) Projection.**

To distinguish Third Angle from the original unnamed projection method it is compulsory to state the fact on each drawing. There are two ways of doing this, see Fig.22.

**THIRD ANGLE PROJECTION       or**

**Fig.22. Two Ways of Stating Third Angle Projection.**

As First Angle Projection is obsolete, all new designs should be in Third Angle Projection and each drawing clearly marked with the projection, using either method already described.

Two questions which may be asked can be answered here.

• Why are Second and Fourth Angle Projections not used? The answer is that the Elevation would lie on top of, or underneath, the Plan and so cause confusion.

- Why has Third Angle Projection superseded First Angle Projection? The answer lies in Fig.23 which shows Third Angle Projection of the block with an Isometric Projection of it alongside. It will be seen that it is much easier to visualise the block as a solid when Third Angle Projection is used.

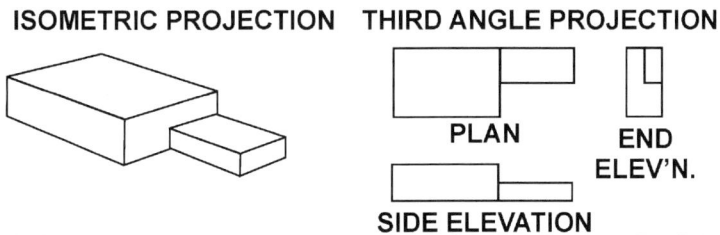

**Fig.23. Isometric and Third Angle Projection.**

AutoCAD's 3D engine is not generally used for routine, or 'Orthographic', drawing work in industry, but is used for illustrations in instruction and maintenance manuals, and in workshop drawing books. It is, however, the method used for 3D printing in which a solid plastic object can be made directly from a 3D image, although it takes some time to obtain the finished result. 3D printing is an additive method of making a component by building it up in layers, whereas most workshop methods are subtractive by removing unwanted material.

## TOLERANCES.

It is physically impossible to make anything to an exact size, and an allowance must be made for this, i.e. engineers must 'tolerate' an error in sizing. This is why every drawing must specify tolerances, either by a general tolerance usually stated at the bottom of the drawing, and/or specific tolerances directly linked to individual dimensions.

Every stated dimension has an associated tolerance whether specific to that dimension or general to the whole drawing. However an unspecified dimension does not carry a tolerance. Fig.24 gives three different diagrams for applying a tolerance to a dimension.

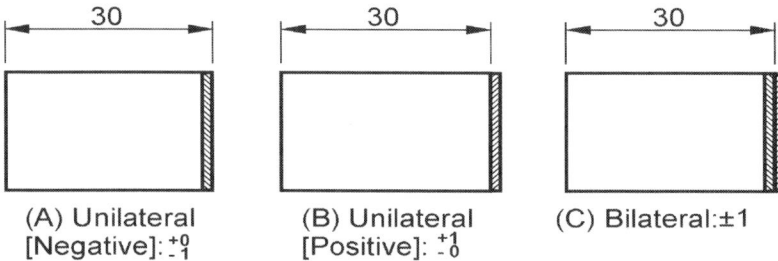

(A) Unilateral [Negative]: $^{+0}_{-1}$     (B) Unilateral [Positive]: $^{+1}_{-0}$     (C) Bilateral:±1

**Fig.24. Tolerance Methods.**

**Diagram A:** The tolerance is negative unilateral. It allows the dimension to vary between the stated [or 'nominal'] size ('+0') and 1 mm less ('-1') so the finished part must measure between 39 and 40 millimetres. It must not go beyond either or it will fail inspection (meaning it will need correcting or scrapping). If oversize it can be corrected, but not if undersize.

**Diagram B:** The tolerance is positive unilateral. This allows the part to vary between the nominal size ('-0') and 1mm more ('+1'). So when finished it must measure between 40 and 41 millimetres, but not beyond either.

**Diagram C:** The tolerance is bilateral, i.e. both positive and negative. If it is ±1 it lies between ('+1') and ('-1'), so the finished part must measure between 39 and 41 millimetres and not beyond either, although it is preferable to make it as near 40 millimetres as possible. No self-respecting craftsman will accept second-best. If he goes beyond the tolerance he will prefer to remake the part and not 'bodge', and it will be quicker in the end. Time taken at the start to get the job right (equivalent to making a solid foundation), will save much time, trouble, and possibly expense, later.

He will know that if the details are right, then the assembly will look after itself. The tolerance of ±1 will allow the part to be made within the cost allowed, but if the tolerance were tightened to ±0.005mm (0.0002") then the time taken to make and check the part will. be greatly extended and the cost will increase sharply, see Fig.25

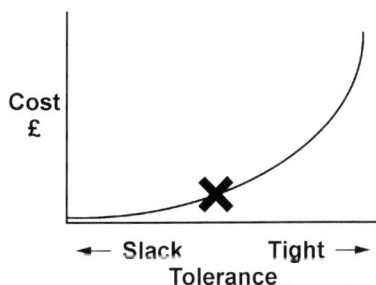

**Fig.25. Graph of Cost v Tolerance.**

The draughtsman or CAD operator will need to choose his

tolerance level carefully. Too tight and the cost of the part will be too high; too slack and the part may not fit the assembly or even work properly.

## AIDS TO PROJECTION

There is no shame in using very thin lines to project an elevation from a plan. Even competent designers wielding pencils would do it to ensure the correct sizes were being transferred to the elevation, and they would erase the guide lines after the elevation was completed.

The same thing can occur in CAD, but the removal of the guide lines is by using the DELETE key.

End elevations can be drawn with lines projecting from both plan and side elevation. There are two ways of turning these lines through 90°, as shown in Fig.26. The example is taken from Fig.21. Here the lines are projected towards the viewing point from the plan and side elevation.

**Left:** Radii have been drawn through 90° to place the projected lines where the elevation is to be drawn and projection lines are carried upwards from the radii. The centre of the radii need not line on either a horizontal or vertical projection line.

**Right:** Where the end elevation is to be placed, a line is drawn vertically down to meet the line from the bottom of the side

elevation. Where these lines intersect, a line is drawn at 45° towards the plan. The horizontal lines above the base line will intersect with the sloping line, and where they intersect vertical lines are drawn.

A grid of lines now occupies the space where the end elevation is to be placed, and the proper outlines can now be drawn upon the grid, after which the projecting lines and the sloping line are erased.

Note. If any other angle is used for the line instead of 45°, the height of the end elevation will vary accordingly. Only 45° guarantees the correct size.

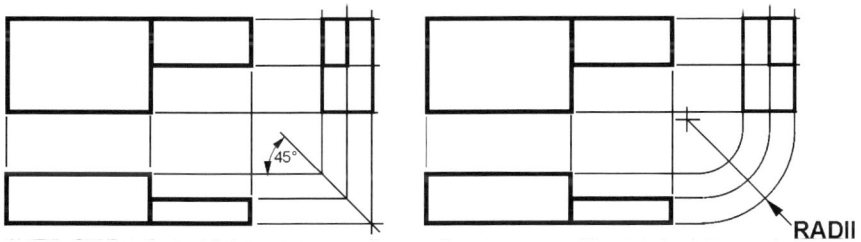

**Fig.26. Projecting Lines for Another View.**

## SCALING.

Where a component is physically bigger than the drawing sheet it will be necessary to scale it down, i.e. reduce it to a size which will fit the sheet.

In Imperial the preferred reduction scales are 1:2, 1:4, 1:8, etc.

Non-preferred reductions are 1:3, 1:6, 1:7, and 1:9, etc.

In Metric the preferred scales are 1:2, 1:5, and 1:10, etc. but these are relatively big steps and non-preferred ratios, e.g. 2:5, are often used.

There are some components when drawn full size are too small to allow all the necessary information about them to be included. So they are scaled up, or enlarged, to fit the sheet. Preferred enlargements are 2:1, 4:1, 5:1, and 10:1. In pencil drawing care has to be taken to draw everything to the same scale, and scale rulers may be found useful for this purpose.

Scaling in CAD is relatively easy, by boxing, or 'marqueeing', the projections and altering the overall dimensions to the scale required. The preferred increases or decreases should correspond to those given above. ModelSpace should be used to keep the lines at a consistent width.

## ABBREVIATIONS.

It is not necessary on a drawing to spell all the words in full, as there are a number of abbreviations in common use, and these are seen in Fig.27.

If non-listed abbreviations are used the workshop may demand an explanation.

| ABBREV. | FULL MEANING |
|---------|-------------|
| Ø | Diameter [Alt + 0216 on keypad]. |
| ^ | Datum [Shift + 6]. |
| A/C | Across corners. |
| A/F | Across flats |
| Approx. | Approximately. |
| C'Bore. | Counterbore. |
| Chfr. | Chamfer. |
| Crs. | Centre Distance. |
| CSK. | Countersink. |
| Ctrs. | Centre Distance. |
| Dia. | Diameter. |
| Elev'n. | Elevation. |
| Eff. | Effective. |
| $f$ | Finish machine [Alt + 0131 on keypad]. |
| F.S. | Full Size. |
| Hex. | Hexagon. |
| Max. | Maximum. |
| Min. | Minimum. |
| O/All | Overall. |
| No. | Number |
| P.C.D. | Pitch Circle Diameter. |
| Qty. | Quantity. |
| R. | Radius. |
| Rad. | Radius. |
| Ref. | Reference. |
| Sq. | Square. |
| Th'd. | Thread |
| Thk. | Thick. |
| Tol. | Tolerance. |
| Thro' | Through |
| Thru' | Through. |

**Fig.27. Table of Common Abbreviations.**

# CHAPTER 3.

## GOOD AND BAD DIMENSIONING PRACTICE.

Many drawings, especially in technical magazines and workshop drawing manuals, contain bad practices. The reason is that they are invariably dimensioned without consideration of the effects of the associated tolerances. In such cases neither the author who selected the illustrations, nor the people who actually drew them, understood the rules of dimensioning

## DIMENSIONAL FLOW.

Few engineers seem to grasp the idea that dimensions 'flow' away from the datums. If a block is placed with its datum on a marking out table, it is clear that dimensioning into the table is not possible, so all dimensions must flow upwards from the datum (i.e. marking out is upwards). Similarly with a left hand datum, which is the norm, the dimensions will flow to the right.

## DOUBLE DIMENSIONING.

The form of poor dimensioning which highlights this ignorance of dimensional flow is shown in Fig.28, and it acts like a neon sign saying: **Beware! Technical Ignoramus at work here.** It means that the drawing's creator needs to be trained in dimensioning and tolerances.

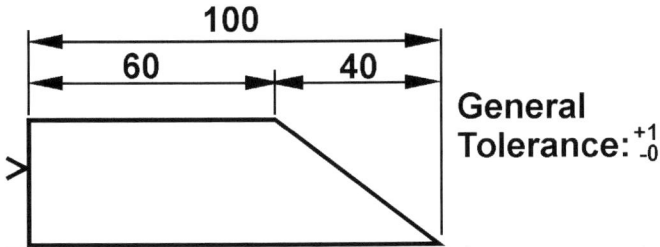

**Fig.28. Double Dimensioning.**

In this diagram the general tolerance is +1, -0, and there is an overall length of 100. Then there is the angle which has a length of 40, and the adjacent side has a length of 60, so these two add up to 100. What has not been taken into account is what happens when the full tolerance is applied to each dimension, see Fig.29, which shows these dimensions in the form of elastic material whose lengths are as given on the drawing.

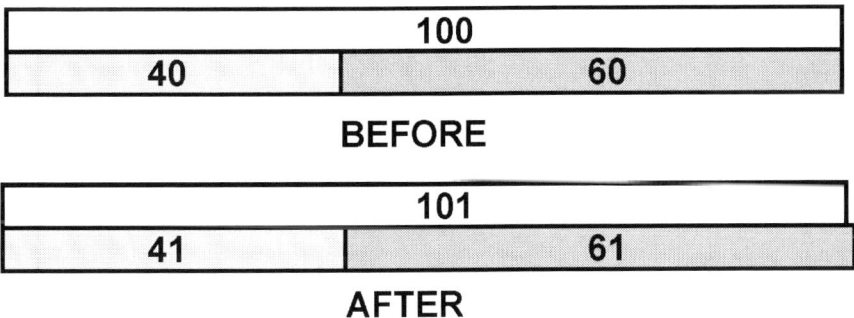

**Fig.29. Dimensional Flow.**

At the top of the diagram they have to same dimensions as in Fig.28, where the full unilateral positive tolerance of -0,+1 applies to each one. At the bottom of the diagram they had the same dimensions with the full positive unilateral tolerance of +1 added to each one, and the right hand end has moved, or 'flowed', away from the left hand end, which is the datum. The overall length has increased to 101, the angle length has increased to 41, and the side to 61, so all are within the drawing tolerance. Meanwhile the combined lengths of the angle and side are 102, and this falls outside the tolerance.

## Double Dimensioning contains a conflict, so it creates an impossible situation that will need resolving.

Only one of the two sets of dimensions can be used, and it is far better to use the overall dimension of 100. Note that if the tolerance is a negative unilateral one of +0, -1 then the dimensions will shorten to 99, 39, and 59 respectively but the effect will be the same.

So how can the side and angle be dimensioned? Solving this dilemma means selecting which is more important between the angle or the side, as shown in Fig.30.

It does not matter what the length of the unimportant non-dimensioned part is, but if a size is to be put on what is left then it must have the word 'reference' after the figure (i.e. not to be used for manufacture, but only as a guide, viz. '24 Ref.'). Aspects with no dimensions are not checked by inspection,

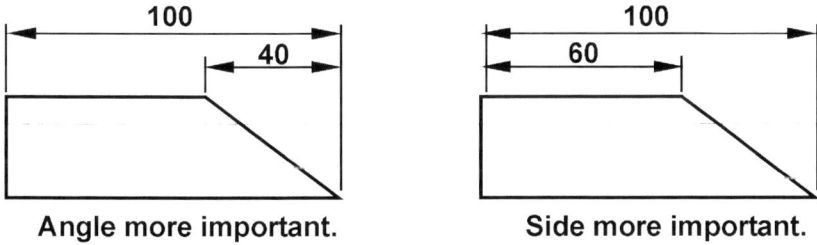

Angle more important.        Side more important.

**Fig.30. Solving the Dilemma.**

In this figure the unimportant aspect is allowed to drift, and its length will be the difference between the other two dimensions, but since this part contains an angle the method of giving its size is shown in Fig.31.

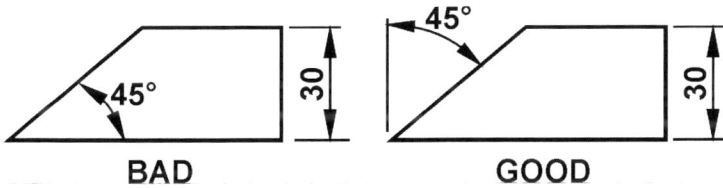

BAD                    GOOD

**Fig.31. Dimensioning an Angle.**

But what happens if both the side and the angle require dimensions? The answer is to show them so, but then the overall length needs to be given as a reference size. It is bad practice to place dimensions or notes upon the component. There is a place for dimensions and notes, and they are OUTSIDE the outline. The only things which should be written on the component are those letters and numbers which are stamped or marked upon it. A good example of this is a fascia plate, upon which written dimensions could be mistaken for markings.

## GOOD AND BAD PRACTICE.

When it comes to linear dimensions there are bad and good practices, and the bad ones occur frequently. Fig.32 left shows a way of showing a centre line position that many draughts people think is clever, but they are wrong.

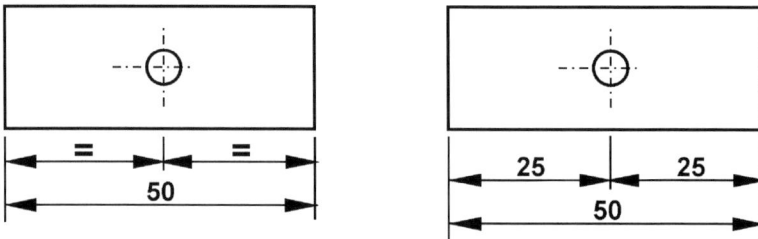

**Fig.32. Dimensioning a Centre Lne.**

On the right is really what they are writing on the drawing. It is double dimensioning, which shows their technical ignorance. Only one of those '25' dimensions is needed.

One of the worst dimensional methods is shown in Fig.33.

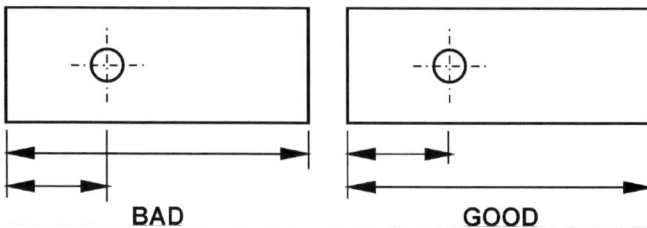

**Fig.33. Crossing Dimension Lines.**

The left hand elevation shows projection lines crossing a dimension line. This shows a lack of planning, and falls foul of good presentation. It is much better to have the dimensions as indicated in the right hand view. This theme is continued in Fig.34.

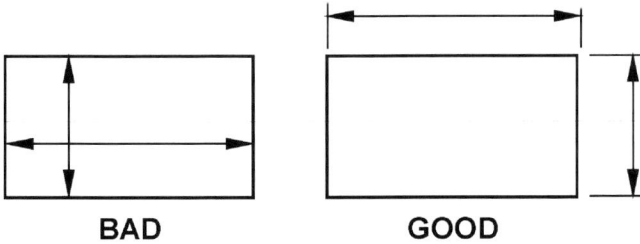

BAD              GOOD

**Fig.34. Crossed and Open Dimension Lines.**

In the left hand view, the bad practice of crossing dimension lines has been compounded by the equally bad practice of placing them on the component, and this should be avoided at all costs. The right hand view shows the correct way of dimensioning the part.

Dimensioning of hatched sections is shown in Fig.35.

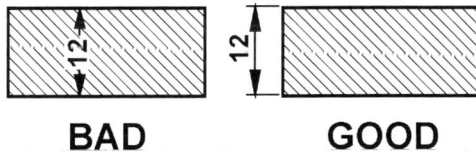

**BAD             GOOD**

**Fig.35. Dimensioning a Hatched Section.**

In the left hand view the dimension has been superimposed on the hatched section. This is bad practice because:

(a) it has been placed on the part, and

(b) that it is almost illegible against the hatching.

The correct method of doing this is shown in the right hand view.

Fig.36 shows good and bad practice in inserting dimension numbers.

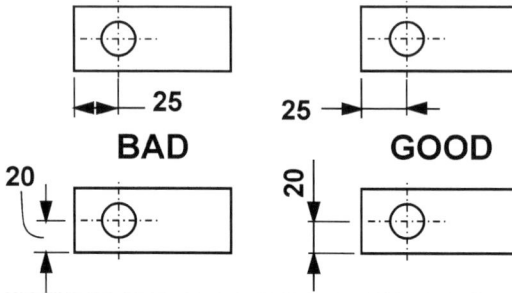

**Fig.36. Direct and Indirect Dimension Figures.**

On the left hand view the figure has been inserted with an indirect line because there was not enough room between the projection lines, but it is a vertical dimension so the number should read from the right and not from the bottom. It shows a lack of knowledge of presentation and of planning the dimensioning, pointing to incompetence. The right hand view shows how it should be done.

Fig.37 shows a part with a chamfer on one corner.

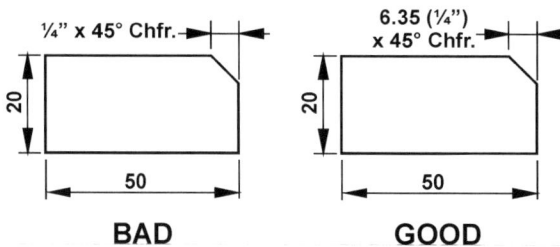

**Fig.37. Combined Measuring Systems.**

In the left hand view the part is dimensioned in metric but the chamfer is dimensioned in imperial. This is taboo as the two systems must not be used together on the same drawing because there may not be both sets of measuring equipment in the workshop.

If using metric, then imperial sizes are shown as their metric equivalent, with the imperial size shown in parentheses (round brackets).

If using imperial, then metric sizes are shown with their imperial equivalent and the metric size shown in parentheses.


## SECTIONS.

These are used to reveal hidden parts that may be difficult to see properly on an elevation. A plan of an assembly with welded blocks, each with a through hole, is shown in Fig.38.

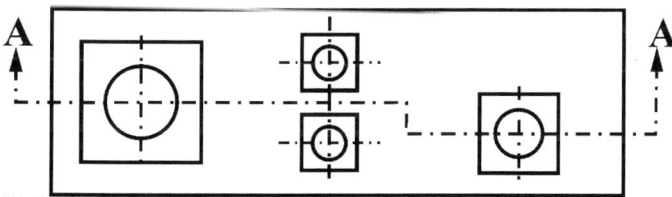

**Fig.38. Plan of Plate with 4 Blocks.**

The section line has two letters '**A**' that indicate the viewing position is at the bottom of the plan., and is shown in Fig.39.

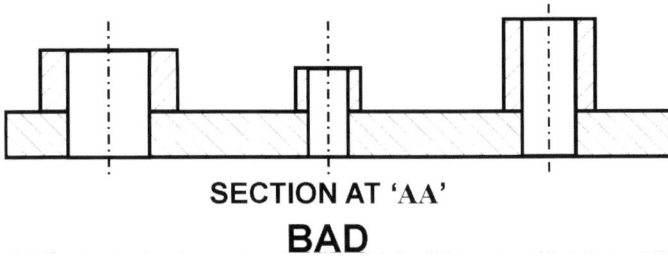

SECTION AT 'AA'
## BAD

**Fig.39. Incorrect Section on 'AA' of Plate with 4 Blocks.**

It shows bad practice, because the section line cuts through the centres of the outer two blocks with their through holes but not through the rear centre block and hole, yet these are shown sectioned. Items behind the section line should be shown in full. The block in front of the line is ignored.

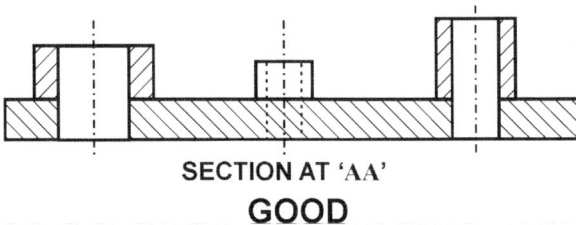

SECTION AT 'AA'
## GOOD

**Fig.40. Correct Section on 'AA' of Plate with 4 Blocks.**

The correct section is shown in Fig.39. The centre block and its hole are not sectioned, because they lie behind the section line (i.e. what is seen if the part was to be sawn along the section line).

Dimensioning a fairly thin part is shown in Fig.41. In the left hand view the arrowheads have been placed inside the projection lines, but there is so little room that they are almost touching each other, and the dimension line itself is hardly visible. This is defeating the purpose of the dimension line.

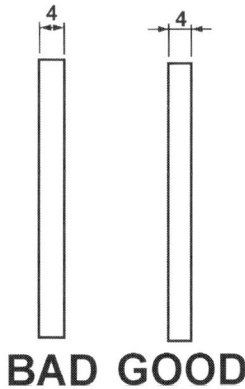

**Fig.41. Dimensioning a Fairly Thin Part.**

It is better to put the arrowheads outside the projection lines but pointing inwards, so the size can be placed upon the dimension line, as shown in the right hand view.

Dimensioning a very thin part is shown in Fig.42 where in on the left the arrowheads are outside the projection lines, but there is not enough room between the projection lines to write the number.

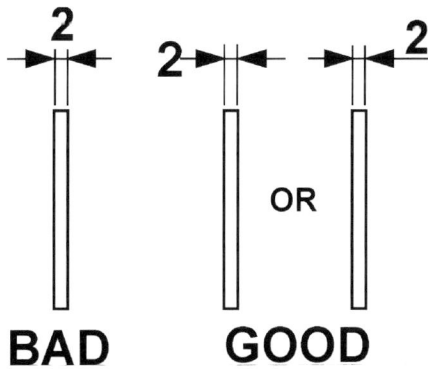

**Fig.42. Dimensioning a Very Thin Part.**

In this case the number should be written alongside, or just above, the external dimension line on whichever side is convenient. If the number is written on top of the line it is also good practice to extend the dimension line to just past the written size, as shown in the right hand view.

Dimensioning a laminate assembly is shown in Fig.43.

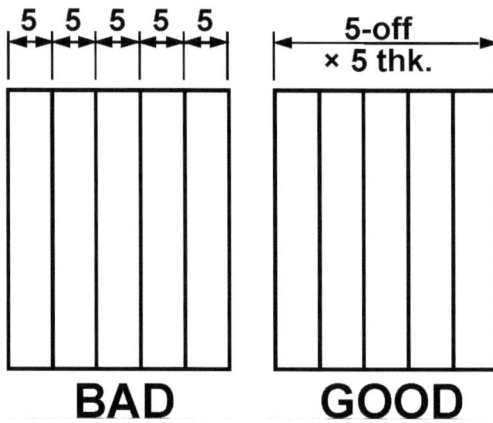

**Fig.43. Dimensioning a Laminate Assembly.**

In the left hand assembly each laminate has been dimensioned, but contains the same bad practice as in Fig.44 above. In such cases it is better to dimension across the assembly and put a block figure "X-off @ Y thick", as shown in the right hand view.

Dimensioning a radius is shown in Fig.44.

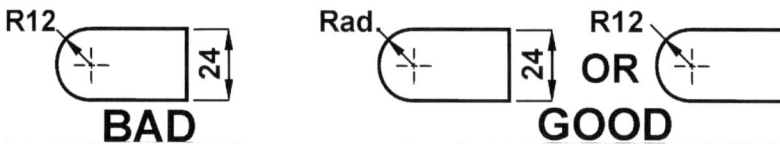

## Fig.44. Dimensioning a Radius.

In the left hand view the radius has been dimensioned as well as the width of the part. As the radius is half of the diameter the result is double dimensioning which is bad practice. The same tolerance is applied to both the width and the radius, but as the radius is half the diameter, the diameter will end up with twice the tolerance even though it is nominally the same size as the width.

It is better to give the width and merely indicate the curve as 'Radius', or else dimension the radius and ignore the width, as shown in the right hand view.

Where separate components have to be fastened to another component to form an assembly, the holes in the parts must correspond with the holes in the mating parts, see Fig.45.

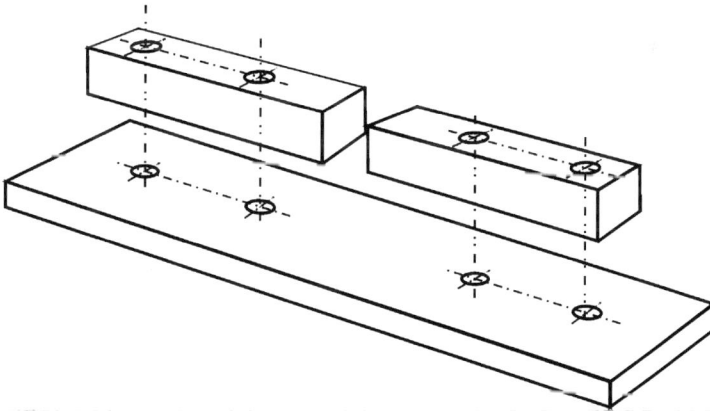

## Fig.45. Two Blocks to be Fastened to a Plate.

The holes in each block are linked and controlled by centre

distances, as are the mating holes in the plate. But as the two blocks are independent of each other, the holes in the plate between them are not linked.

The way of dimensioning sets of linked holes is shown in Fig.46.

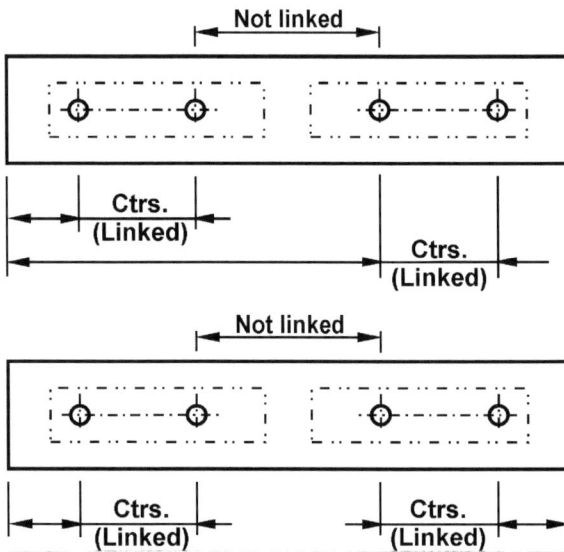

**Fig.46. Dimensioning Sets of Linked Holes.**

## ASSEMBLIES.

An assembly which has been dimensioned is shown in Fig.47. In the left hand view the assembly is sectioned on the centre line, and both the block and the bush have been dimensioned. This is bad practice as it defies the BSI Kitemark requirements which are covered in Chapter 7.

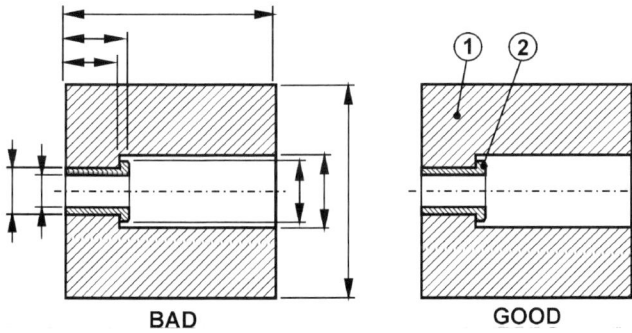

## Fig.47. Dimensioning an Assembly.

On each assembly drawing the individual parts should be ballooned, as shown in the right hand view, and a separate Item List compiled. Each part may then be drawn as a detail on its own drawing sheet. The only measurements suitable for an assembly drawing are reference dimensions, to save having to look through the detail drawings for the information, and setting dimensions where an operation cannot be performed before the assembly stage.

Please Note! Reference dimensions which are sometimes seen on more complex drawings are purely mathematical computations used for checking purposes and are generally a 'ball-park' figure. They are not an actual dimension and it is taboo to use them as such.

## 'CUMULATIVE' AND 'NON-CUMULATIVE' DIM'NS.

There are two methods to dimension any component, and these are called 'Cumulative' and 'Non-cumulative' respectively. It is quite common for both types to be used on the same drawing, although each will have a different effect upon the component, or more accurately, their tolerances will. Each tolerance can be specific to the dimension, if not the general tolerance is used. Although only hole positions will be considered, the rules apply to any object on the drawing.

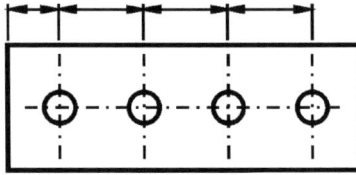

**Fig.48. Cumulative Dimensioning.**

In Fig.48 the left hand hole is the datum and the other holes are dimensioned from it. These holes are linked, usually with a stated centre distance. As each dimension has its own tolerance the result over all the holes is the sum of all the tolerances. This method of dimensioning is called **'garlanding'.**

A 'Pitch Circle Diameter' with 6 holes is shown in Fig.49.

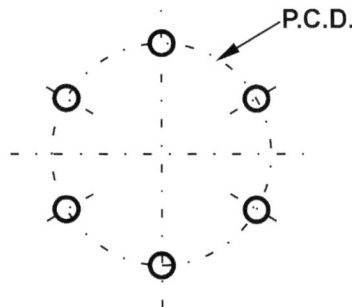

**Fig.49. Pitch Circle Diameter.**

The distance between each pair of holes is called a 'Pitch', which can be linear or circular. 'Circle' means that the holes are all on a circle, and 'Diameter' means the diameter of the circle with the holes on it. Holes on a P.C.D. are all cumulatively dimensioned.

In Fig.50 each hole is individually dimensioned from the datum and there is no measurement between holes, so they are not linked. Because each hole is directly connected to the datum it has its own independent tolerance and so the tolerances are not cumulative. Because each hole is directly connected to the datum it has its own tolerance and as a result the tolerances are not cumulative. This method of dimensioning is called 'cascading'.

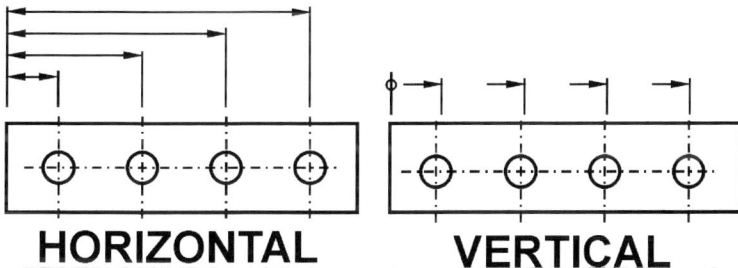

**HORIZONTAL**   **VERTICAL**

**Fig.50. Non-Cumulative Dimensioning.**

It is usually space consuming but 'vertical cascading', seen in the right hand view, can be used in certain circumstances.

When a hole or a block, or any other feature, has a dimension to it the dimension is a nominal figure (the one aimed for), but during manufacture of the component that dimension may 'grow' by the addition of, or 'shrink' by the subtraction of, the tolerance. That means the hole or other component can actually move in relationship with the origin of the dimension, and this is where the flow of dimensions will be of use. With a positive tolerance the feature will flow away from the point of origin, and with a negative tolerance it will flow towards the point of origin.

## SCREW THREADS.

Over the years the representation of screw threads has changed. Fig.51 shows the changes for a square head screw and its mating hole, seen in section.

Old drawings used the method at Fig.51 (left), later drawings used the method at Fig.51 (middle). Note the method of denoting a square or flat. Drawings now use the method at Fig.51 (right), as it is quicker and just as effective.

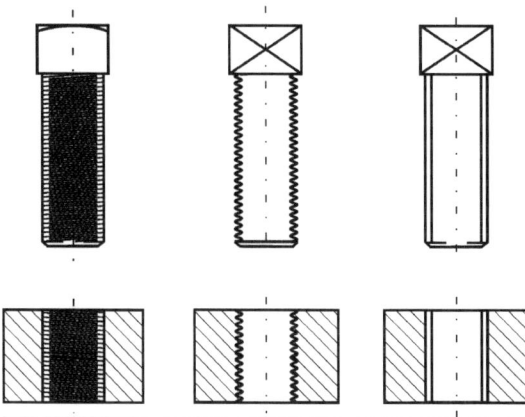

**Fig.51. Development in the Method of Showing Screw Threads.**

## DESIGN PROTECTION.

Every designer should try to look ahead and anticipate any problems which might arise on his drawing. The sign given in Fig.52 should be above every drawing board and CAD station.

# THINK AHEAD

**Fig.52. The Reminder Notice**.

The designer's task is to establish whether each component will be acceptable upon completion if any, or all, of the dimensions end up with the full tolerance on them, i.e. a dimension of 40.00 with a +1/-0 tolerance can end anywhere between 40.00 and 41.00 and would be acceptable, whereas 39.99 and 41.01 would not.

## WORST CASE SCENARIOS (W.C.S.).

The tool used for this purpose is called a 'Worst Case Scenario' which helps designers to ensure that their designs will work correctly in practice, as it highlights adverse tolerance movements. It will become clear how this tool actually functions.

A typical example is given in Fig.53. This plate has a general tolerance of ±1. It is 1 mm thick, and the outside is a 10 mm square. It also has a hole, meant to be in the centre, which is 6mm diameter.

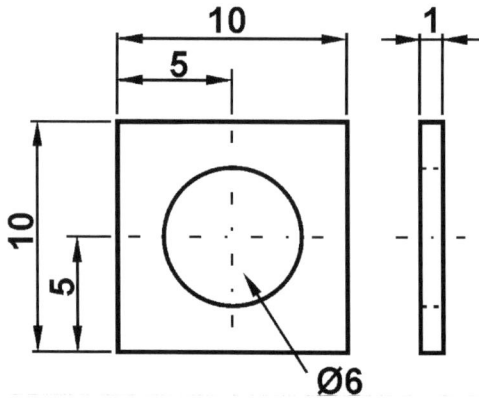

**Fig.53. Small Plate.**

The Best Case Scenario, which is the one expected by the person doing the drawing, is shown in Fig.54.

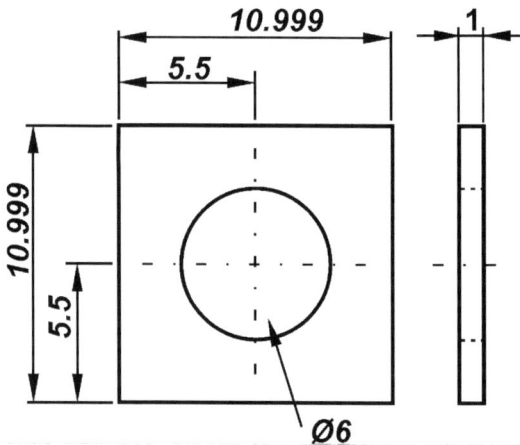

**Fig.54. Small Plate, Best Case Scenario.**

In this the plate has grown to 10.999 square and is still within the tolerance. The hole has obligingly kept almost central with the dimensions to the hole centre increasing by only 0.5, and the hole itself has behaved by staying at Ø6.

To think that will always be the situation is to live in a fool's paradise, as Fig.55 shows with the Worst Case Scenario.

In this Worst Case Scenario the plate has shrunk by 0.999 to 9.001. The hole centre dimensions have similarly shrunk to 4.001 each, and the hole has expanded to Ø6.999.

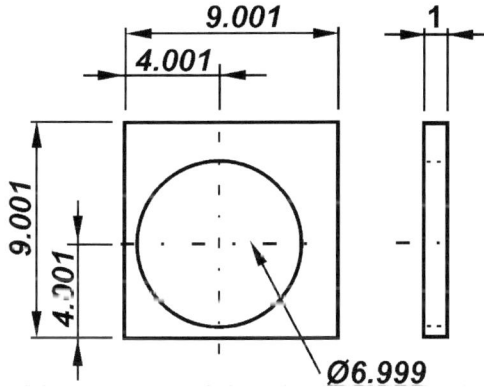

**Fig.55. Small Plate, Worst Case Scenario.**

**All the dimensions are still within the drawing tolerance, and accordingly should be accepted by inspection, but there are other considerations.**

The offset hole may not fit the equipment for which it is intended, and there is only 0.002mm metal between the hole and two edges, which is so thin that the plate will not withstand any force put upon it. Because of that lack of strength the Plate will be rejected and will become scrap metal.

As a rule of thumb: **The centre of the hole should be at least its diameter away from the edge.** Anything less will probably not be strong enough.

The student's task for each of the Exercises given in the next two Chapters will be:

1. To derive the Worst Case Scenario and decide if the finished part will pass inspection;

2. To consider possible ways of changing the design of those items from 1 above which fail inspection so that the new Worst Case Scenario drawn would result in them being acceptable.

# CHAPTER 4.

## 'C' SERIES (CUMULATIVE TOL.) EXERCISES.

**The components given will be dimensioned in a cumulative manner, the tolerance will be stated, as will the amount to which each dimension may extend or shrink.**

In the following examples the maximum error will be +0.999mm, just within the +1/-0 general tolerance. Note that the outside dimensions will not alter although they too will be subject to the drawing tolerances, as the emphasis here is on the holes. Nevertheless the same principles apply to all elements on the drawing.

## DRAWING THE WORST CASE SCENARIOS.

The task is to draw the Worst Case Scenario for each exercise, and decide whether the examples will pass inspection at the end of the operation. To do this it may be advisable to draw the component to scale on paper and place each hole at its dimension plus/minus the full tolerance, e.g. for a dimension of 20 ±1 it can be drawn either as 19 or 21, whichever will give the worse result. As a guide, holes would go bigger and outside shapes smaller. Similar treatment should be given to other relevant dimensions.

The rules are:

1. Dimensions are unilateral, but may be either positive or negative.
2. Dimensions can end with the general tolerance added but less 0.001mm, i.e. in the case above the end result of the 20 dimension with a positive unilateral tolerance would be 20.999, and with a negative unilateral tolerance it would be 19.001.
3. The outside dimensions will not alter.

   Remember that inspection takes account of other factors like thickness of metal remaining, as well as dimensional variations.

**EXERCISE C1.**

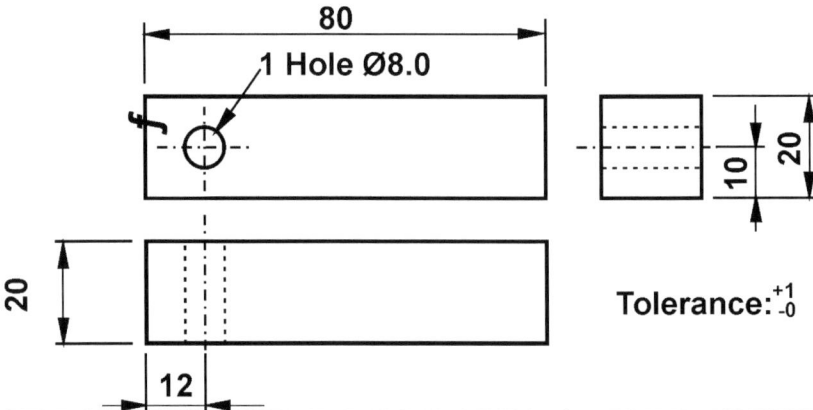

**Fig.56. Block with One Hole.**

**EXERCISE C2.**

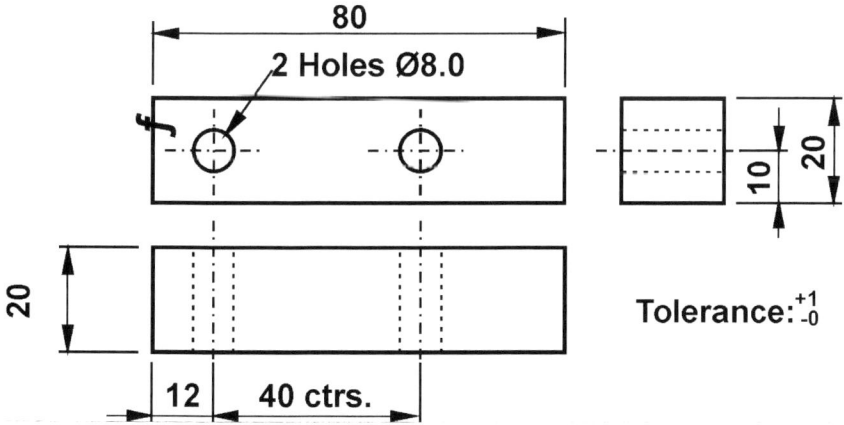

Fig.57. Block with Two Holes.

**EXERCISE C3.**

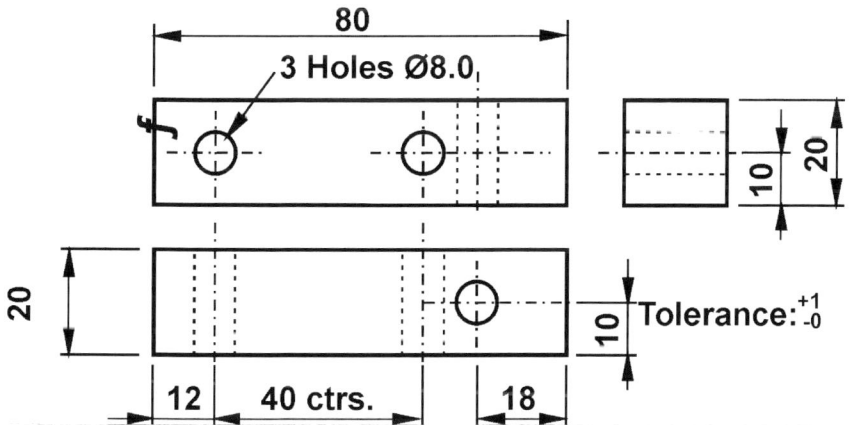

Fig.58. Block with Three Holes.

## EXERCISE C4.

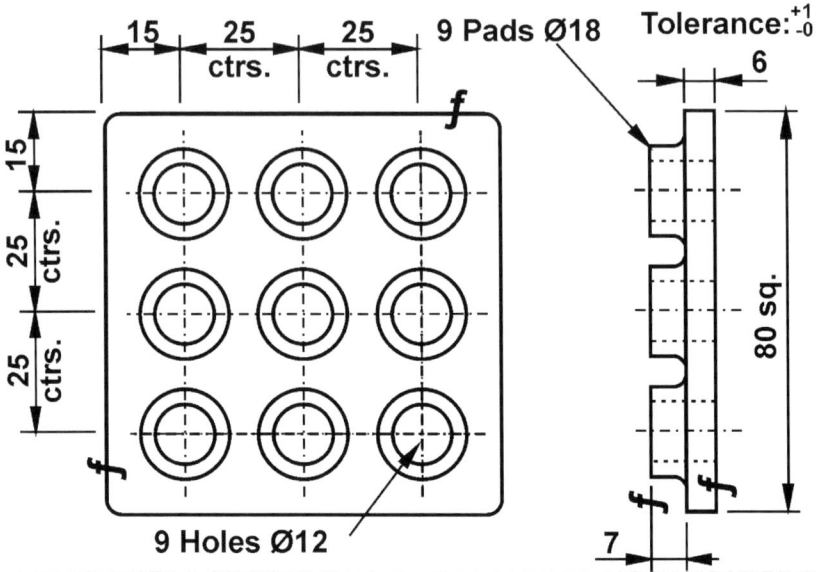

Fig.59. Cast Iron Plate.

## EXERCISE C5.

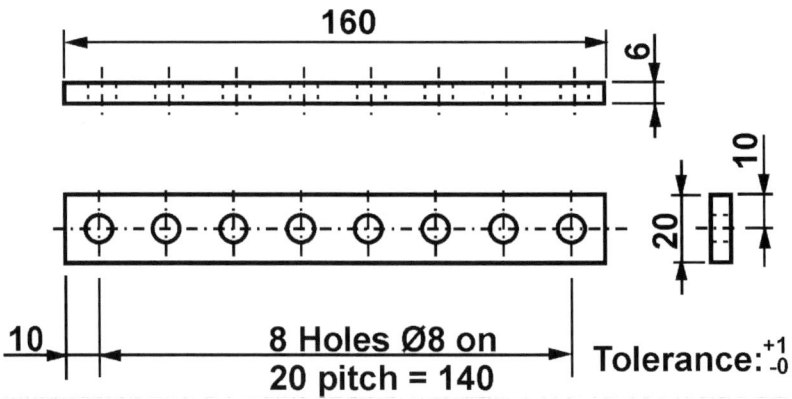

Fig.60. Drilled Strip.

## EXERCISE C6.

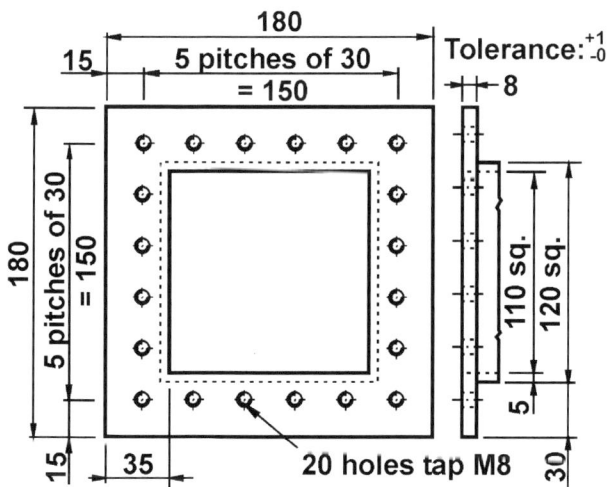

Fig. 61. Ventilation Duct Flange.

## EXERCISE C7.

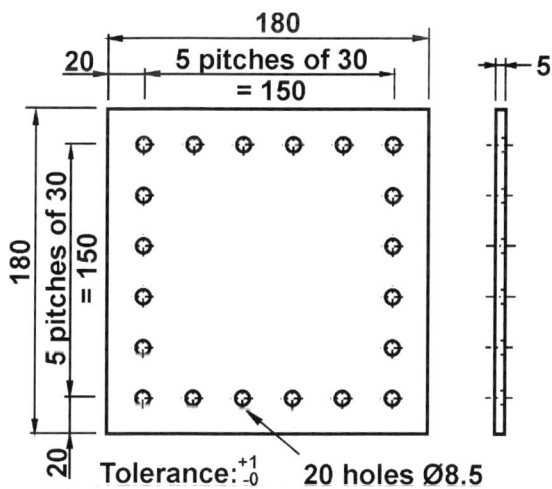

Fig. 62. Duct Flange Blanking Plate.

## EXERCISE C8.

In this exercise the datum is on the left hand side, and the fitter rightly starts at the left hand side.

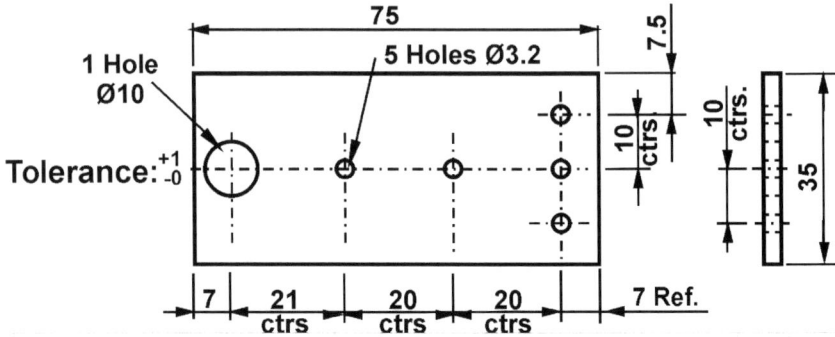

**Fig.63. Small Plate, Working from Datum.**

## EXERCISE C9.

In this exercise the datum is on the right hand side, but the fitter will incorrectly start at the left hand side.

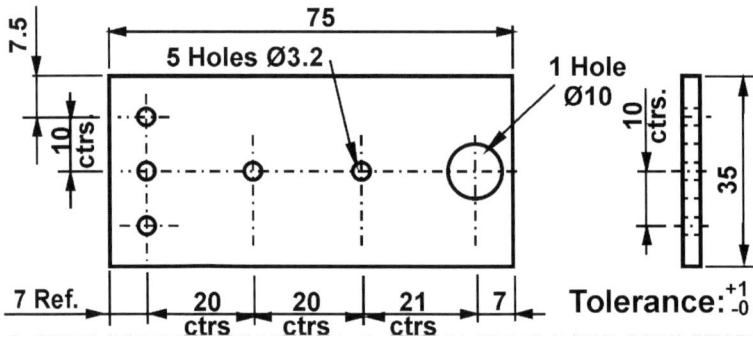

**Fig.64. Small Plate, Working from Reference dimension.**

## EXERCISE C10.

This exercise, seen in Fig.65, is one of angular error instead of linear, as all linear measurements stay the same. The angle subtended at the centre between each pair of holes is 30°. The angular tolerance is +1°,-0°, and the amount of error will be 0.999°. Start at the top hole and work clockwise.

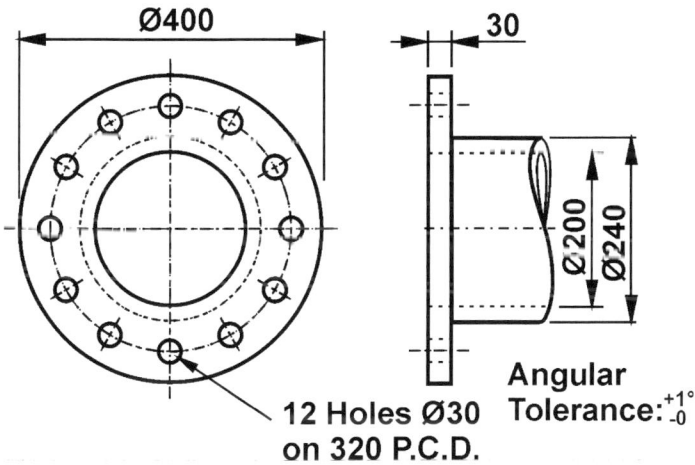

**12 Holes Ø30 on 320 P.C.D.**

Angular Tolerance: $^{+1°}_{-0}$

**Fig.65. Pipe Flange**.

The answers are given in Chapter 9.

# CHAPTER 5.

## 'N' SERIES ( NON-CUMULATIVE TOL.) EXERCISES.

Only 'non-cumulative' dimensions and tolerances will be considered in the 'N' series of exercises which follow. The same conditions will apply as in Chapter 4.

Watch for unexpected movements. It will be necessary to draw the **WORST CASE SCENARIO** and check when the component will pass inspection at the end of the operation.

**EXERCISE N1.**

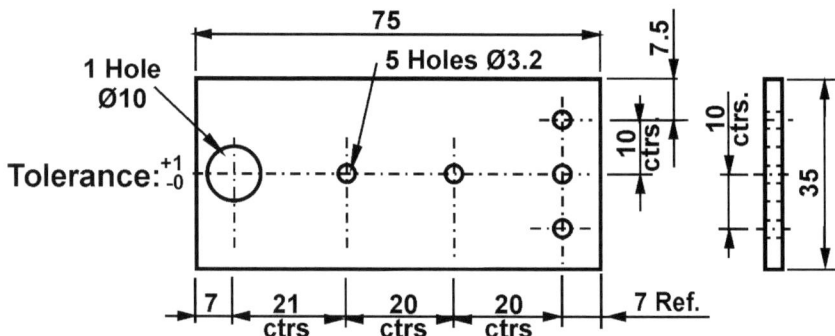

Fig.66. Block with Two Holes.

## EXERCISE N2.

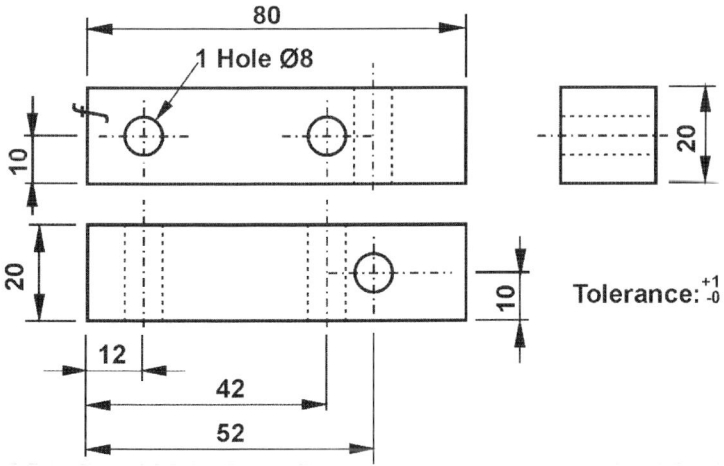

Fig.67. Block with Three Holes.

## EXERCISE N3.

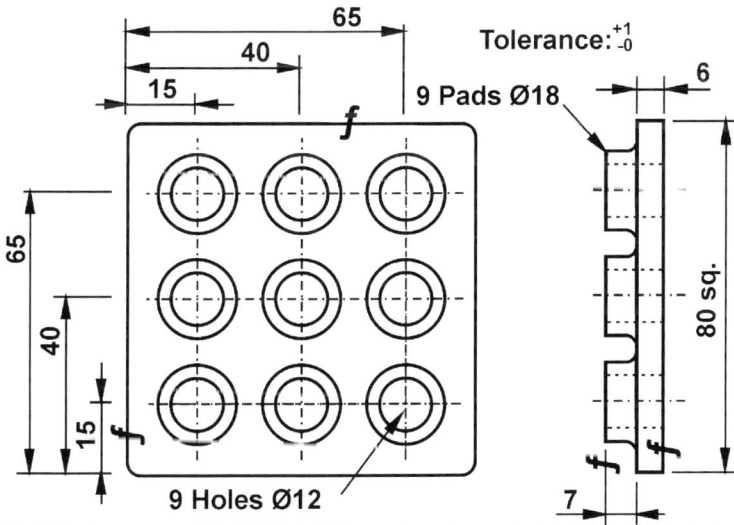

Fig.68. Cast Iron Plate.

**EXERCISE N4.**

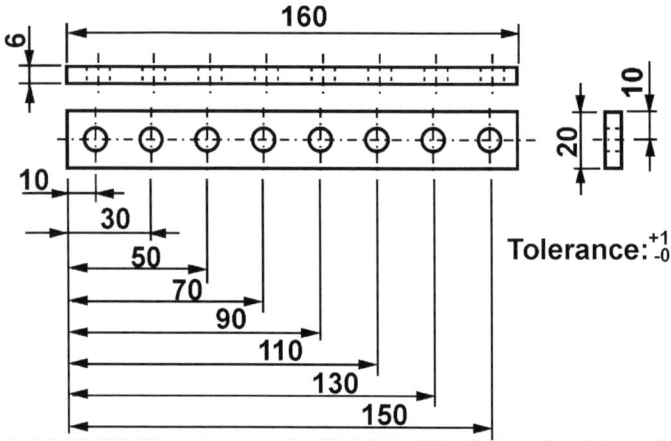

Tolerance: $^{+1}_{-0}$

Fig.69. Drilled Strip.

**EXERCISE N5.**

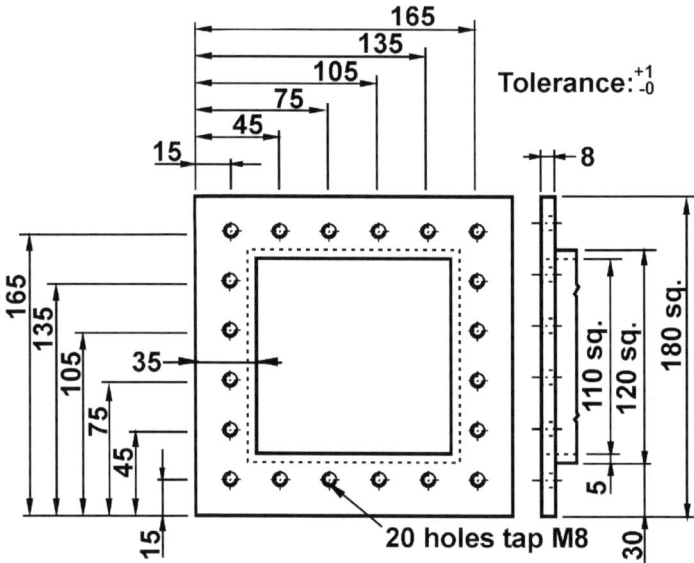

Tolerance: $^{+1}_{-0}$

20 holes tap M8

Fig. 70. Ventilation Duct Flange.

**EXERCISE N6.**

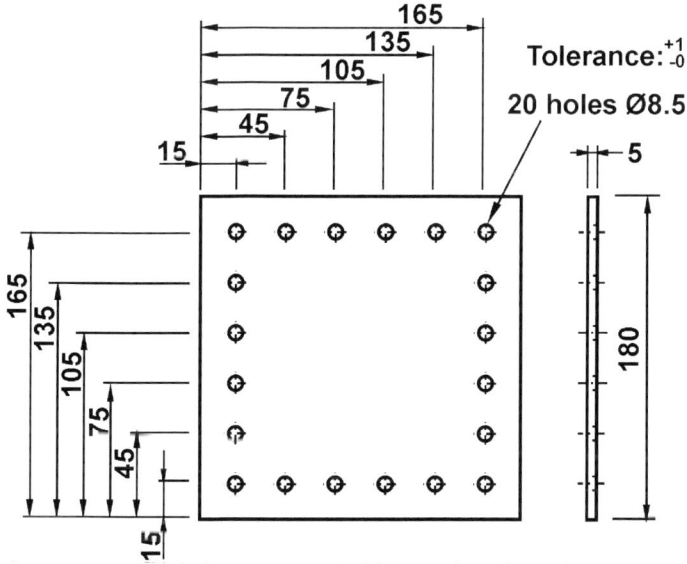

**Fig.71. Duct Flange Blanking Plate.**

**EXERCISE N7.**

In this exercise the datum is on the left hand side and the fitter rightly starts at the left hand side.

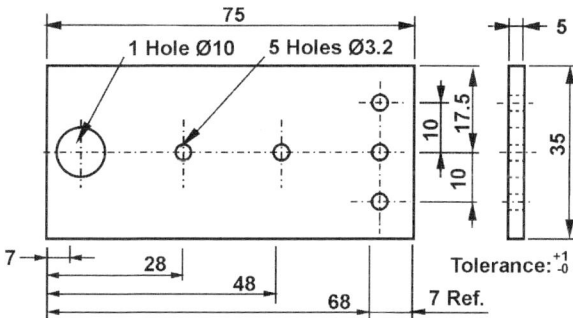

**Fig.72. Small Plate, Working from Datum.**

## EXERCISE N8.

In this exercise the datum is on the right hand side but the fitter incorrectly starts at the left hand side.

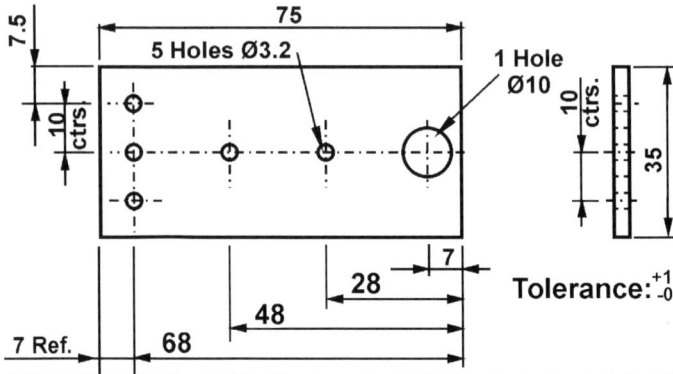

**Fig.73. Small Plate, Working from Reference Dimension.**

## EXERCISE N9.

Non-cumulative dimensions on a P.C.D. are impossible, but there is a way to do it that will minimize the errors.

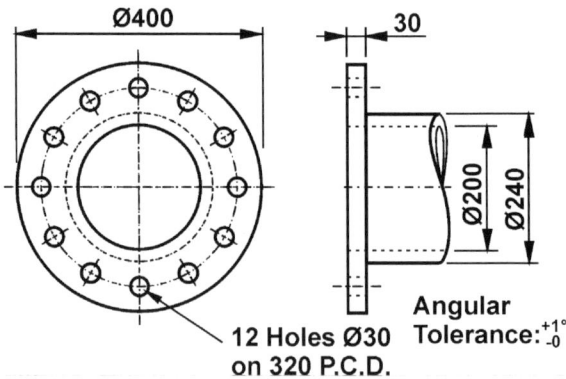

**Fig.74. Pipe Flange.**

In this case a Dividing Head with a gear ratio of 40:1 will be used. The error stated will be applied to the handle but will be reduced by 40 on the component in Fig.74. Rework the exercise using this lesser angular error.

The other way in which the flange holes can be drilled is on a co-ordinate table. A coordinate table works on two axis, and a suitable set dimensions for each axis can be calculated by the use of trigonometry. For three to twelve holes Fig.134 in the Appendix has the necessary information.

The answers to the Exercises are given in Chapter 10.

# CHAPTER 6.

## 'P' SERIES (PRESENTATION) EXERCISES.

These are drawings which have been published but which contain a number of errors and bad practices, although their sources will not be specified as they are examples of 'how-not-to-do-it'.

**The task is to count all the errors on each one, regardless of type of error.** A suggestion is use greaseproof paper over the diagram and mark on that.

**EXERCISE P1.**

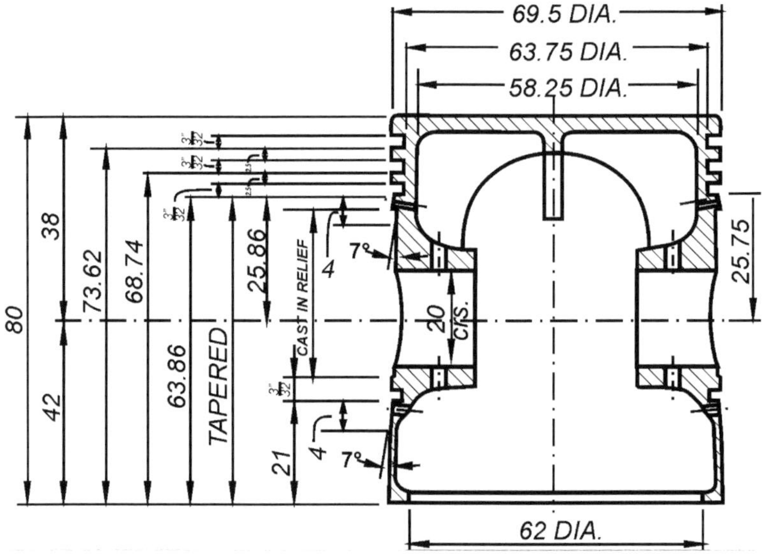

**Fig.75. Piston.**

**EXERCISE P2.**

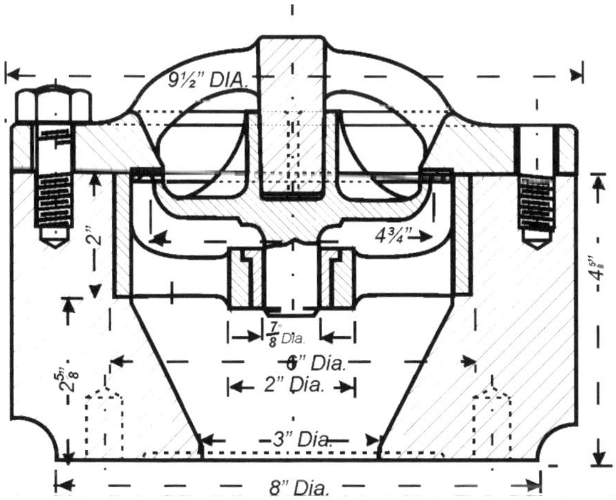

**Fig.76. L.N.E.R. Anti-Vacuum Valve.**

**EXERCISE P3.**

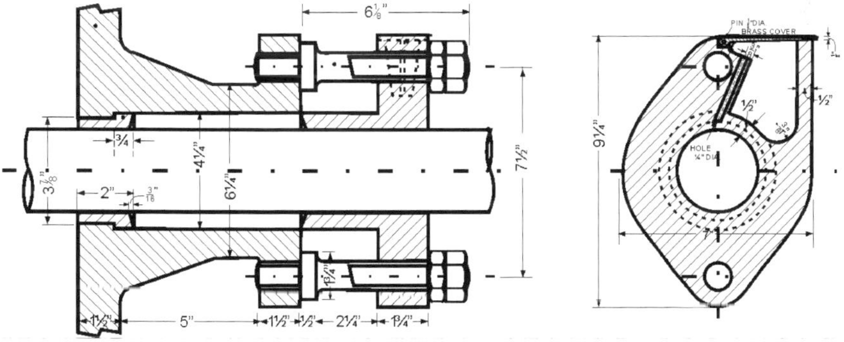

**Fig.77. Horizontal Stuffing Box.**

## EXERCISE P4.

The example in Fig. 77 is in two parts. One was correctly labelled 'Incorrect', and the other wrongly labelled 'Correct'. In fact both contain errors, so they should be treated as two views of the same object. They reveal a distinct lack of knowledge of dimensioning by both the author and his publisher.

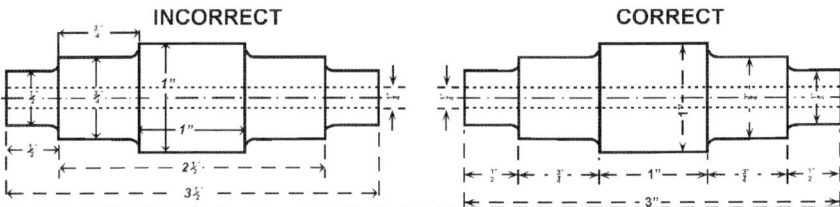

**Fig.78. Stepped Shaft.**

## EXERCISE P5.

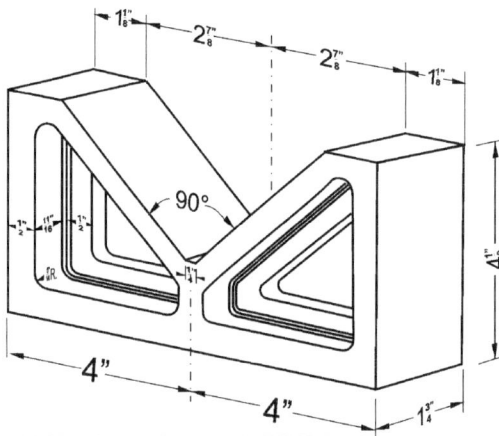

**Fig.79. Vee Block.**

**EXERCISE P6.**

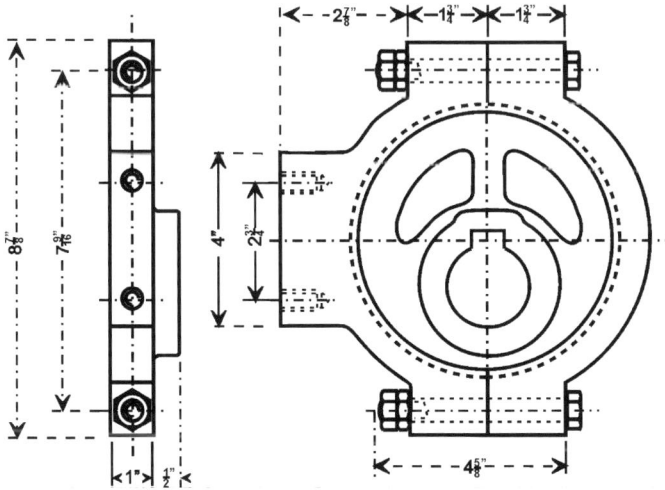

Fig.80. Eccentric Sheave and Strap.

**EXERCISE P7.**

The example in Fig.81 has alphanumeric addenda to the diameters. These are explained in Chapter 7. To make it easier to read, the drawing has been split into two halves and the halves enlarged, see Figs.81A and 80B.

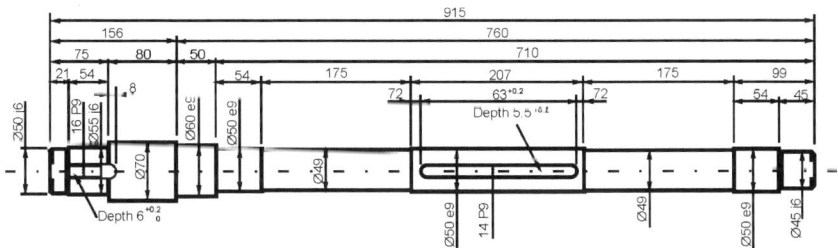

Fig.81. Machine Shaft.

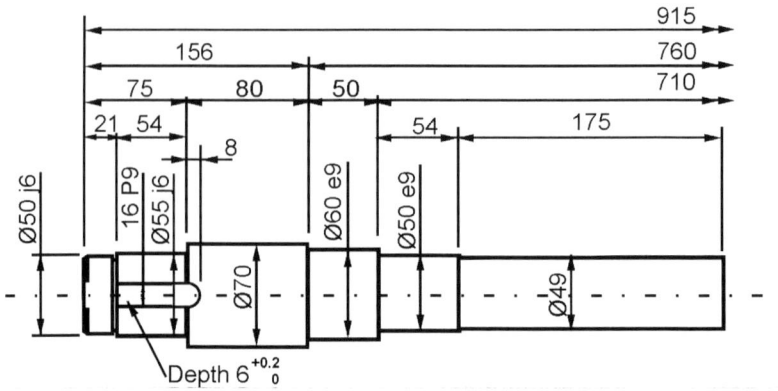

**Fig.81A. Machine Shaft – Left Hand.**

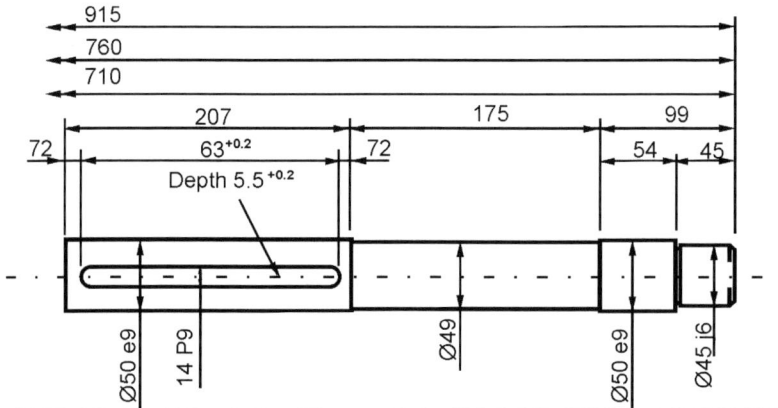

**Fig.81B. Machine Shaft – Right Hand.**

The Answers to the Presentations are given in Chapter 11.

78

# CHAPTER 7.

## LIMITS AND FITS.

Instructions on engineering drawings often describe the fit of a hole and a shaft as 'shrink', 'light press', 'push', 'slide', or 'running'. Just taking one of these, viz. a 'slide fit', the question is: How easy a fit is it? Is it so tight that the shaft will barely move in the hole; so easy it will slip through unless controlled; or is it somewhere between the two?

**They are all vague terms which are open to interpretation. Using them means leaving the decision to the constructor, which is not what the designer should do, and such delegation may give results he did not want.**

In the tool room of a large factory many years ago one of the tool makers was assembling a tool to a drawing and using a bench press to force a dowel of silver steel into a hole that was close to the edge of a hardened steel die block. As he did so the outer skin of the dowel peeled away, but he carried on regardless. The dowel was such a severe fit that eventually the die block cracked along the length of the hole. The drawing had indicated a press fit, and he had applied it. Unfortunately it was the wrong fit. So was the toolmaker at fault? No, he wasn't. There are a range of press fits and the designer should have stated the precise fit he wanted.


## B.S. LIMITS AND FITS.

The correct way to specify fits with their respective limits (or tolerances) in the UK is by using **BSI 1916-1:2009 Limits and Fits for Engineering.** There are a number of parts to this standard, with BS1916–1 being for small sizes, BS1916-2 being for medium sizes and BS1916-3 for large sizes. Only BS1916-1 will be dealt with here. As the array of limits and fits it gives is vast, some guidance is required so that an informed choice can be made.

## BASIC PRINCIPLES.

The limits and fits system is laid out in a grid. Holes use capital letters, viz. 'A' to 'Z', and shafts lower case letters, viz. 'a' to 'z'. There are sixteen grades of fit for both holes and shafts, ranging from 1 to 16. Holes and shafts are denoted by an alphanumeric code, viz, 'C3', or 'y14'.

All these alphanumeric codes have corresponding tolerances which may be found in the associated tables. Grade 1 for both holes and shafts, is the closest fit, and Grade 16 which is the easiest. However, for holes the ranges H7 or H8 are used, as these have unilateral positive tolerances that are easier to produce. The early letters are easy fits, the later letters are for shrink fits.

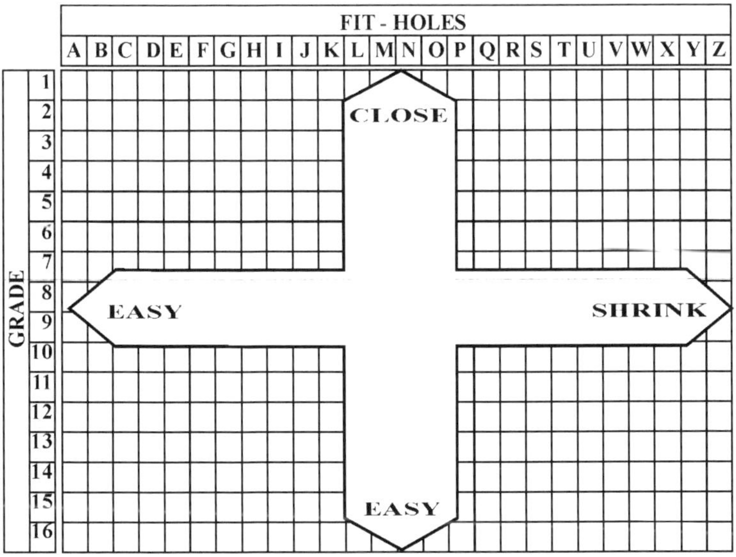

**Fig.82. Tabular Format for Holes.**

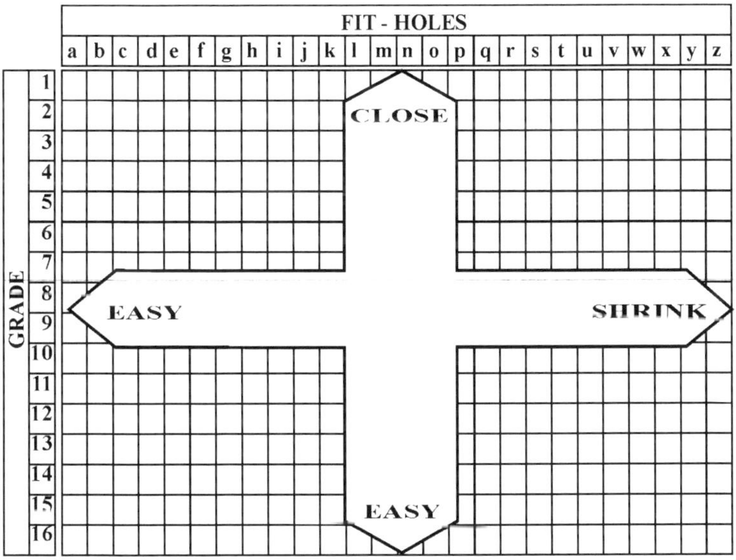

**Fig.83. Tabular Format for Shafts.**

Shafts can range through all of the letters, and 'a' is the smallest and easiest fit. On the other hand 'z' would give a heavy press or shrink fit. A Z1/z1 would be a very close shrink fit, and an A16/a16 a very easy fit, so easy it may well be called a 'rattle' fit. Surface finish is also a factor in the fit, so it will be assumed that the best possible finish is applied to both holes and shafts.

Holes normally have Grade 6 to 8 selected for them, as they have unilateral tolerances which vary according to diameter. The reason is that adjusting the hole size is usually more difficult than adjusting the shaft size. If the hole has a unilateral tolerance then the exact fit will be determined by the shaft tolerance. See Fig.84 - 87 for examples of these fits.

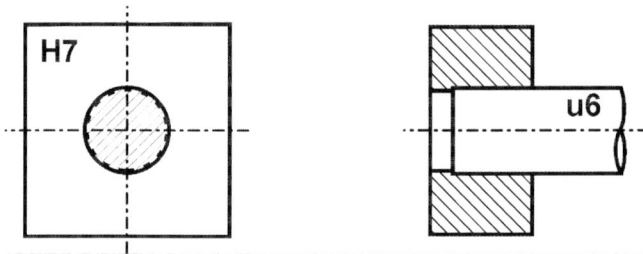

**Fig.84. Shrink Fit.**

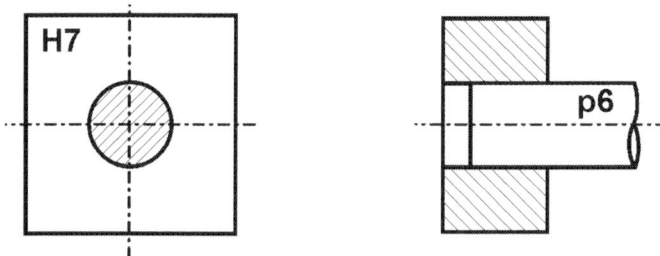

**Fig.85. Press Fit.**

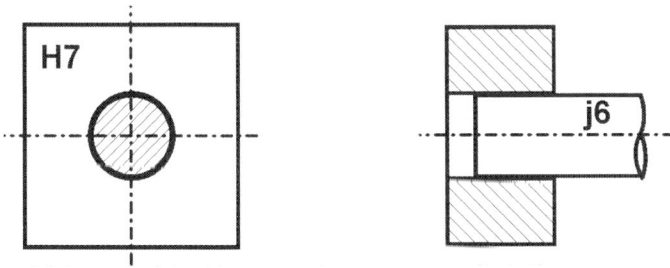

**Fig.86. Push Fit.**

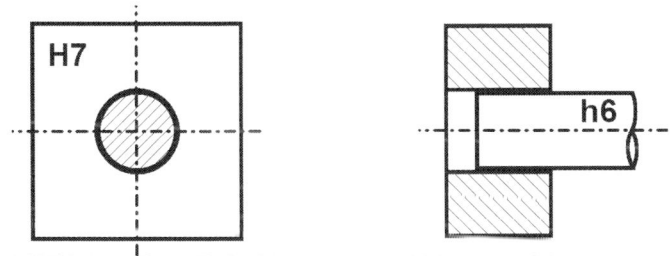

**Fig.87. Slide Fit.**

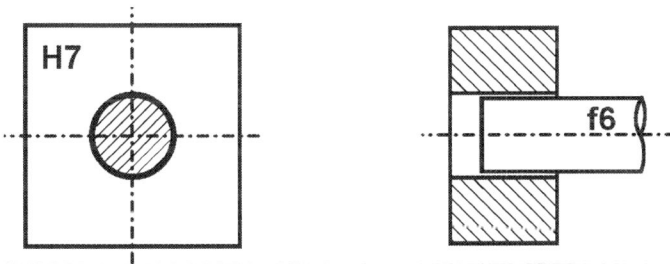

**Fig.88. Running Fit.**

Designers simply write these fits, e.g. H6/j6, on the general assembly drawing by the parts concerned.

Detail draughts people convert these symbols, viz. H6, into the tolerance for the part concerned by looking them up in the appropriate table. The fit symbol may be added afterwards in brackets, e.g. $\varnothing18.00 \ ^{+0.021}_{+0}$ (H7).

Tolerance Tables for Metric and Imperial sizes will be found in the Appendix, and accurate measuring instruments are essential for this work. The nearest Technical College Library should have the Limits and Fits Standard available for examination.

## TOLERANCE EXERCISES.

When choosing a particular fit, the designer may need to know exactly what the best and worst case will be, and this can be achieved by a tolerance exercise. This means that he can determine what the two extremes of tightness and slackness are for the fit he has chosen. An example of a tolerance exercise follows.

A 2" diameter push fit (h7/j6) is required and it is found in the Imperial Table, of which an extract is given in Fig.89.

| NOMINAL SIZES | HOLES BASIC HOLE | SHAFTS | | | | | |
|---|---|---|---|---|---|---|---|
| | | INTERFERENCE | TRANS-ITION | CLEARANCE | | | |
| | | u6 | p6 | j6 | h6 | g6 | f7 |
| OVER - UP TO & INCLUDING | H7 | SHRINK | LIGHT PRESS | PUSH | SLIDE | CLOSE RUN | RUN |
| 1.97 - 2.56 | -.0012 +.0 | +.0042 +.0035 +.0047 +.004 | +.0021 +.0014 | +.0004 +.0003 | +.0 -.0007 | -.0004 -.0011 | -.0012 -.0024 |

## Fig.89. Extract from Imperial Table.

The limits which are not required are ignored, and in Fig.90 the extract is shown without the unwanted figures.

| NOMINAL SIZES | HOLES BASIC HOLE | SHAFTS | | | | | |
|---|---|---|---|---|---|---|---|
| | | INTERFERENCE | | TRANS-ITION | CLEARANCE | | |
| | | u6 | p6 | j6 | h6 | g6 | f7 |
| OVER - UP TO & INCLUDING | H7 | SHRINK | LIGHT PRESS | PUSH | SLIDE | CLOSE RUN | RUN |
| 1.97 - 2.56 | -.0012 +.0 | | | +.0004 +.0003 | | | |

**Fig.90. Abridged Extract from Imperial Table.**

The table gives the hole tolerance as +.0012 and -0, and the shaft tolerance as +.0004 and +.0003. There are two formulae to use to determine the fit.

### (i) Largest Hole Tolerance – Smallest Hole Tolerance.

Taking the largest hole tolerance and subtracting the smallest shaft tolerance, therefore (+.0012) - (+.0003) = .0012 -.0003 = +.0009. **This is .0009 clearance.**

### (ii) Smallest Hole Tolerance – Largest Hole Tolerance.

Taking the smallest hole tolerance and subtracting the largest shaft tolerance, therefore (+0) - (+.0003) = 0 - .0003= -.0003. **This is - .0003 interference.**

If these results are unsatisfactory, a different grade of fit can be taken, say a j4 for a closer fit, or a j8 for a slacker one, but at least by doing this the designer can get the fit he desires.

Tables for both Imperial, up to 7", and Metric, up to 180, are given in the Appendix.

## BEARINGS.

Designs which include bearings need careful consideration of the limits and fits used for installing the bearings. There are four main types of bearing:

- Plain.
- Ball.
- Roller.
- Thrust.

Plain bearings are supplied in a variety of materials, from nylon, through phosphor-bronze to pre-lubricated composites. The bearings will need the housings and the shafts machined to the tolerances specified by the bearing manufacturer. Lubrication methods will also need consideration. If plain bearings are made in-house then the designer will need to select his running fits carefully.

Selection of Ball, Roller, and Thrust bearings will depend upon heat, loading, speed, end thrust, and duty cycle, and they are supplied in a range of degrees of precision.

**The rule for bearing installation is that the rotating ring should have an interference fit, or else be clamped. The static ring merely requires a close fit.**

It is imperative to consult the bearing makers literature for correct application and the fits required for installing the bearings. No recommendations on suitable fits can be given here because the range is so wide.


## DOWELS.

Dowels are used to fix the relationship between two components without fastening them together. They stop one part from sliding sideways in relation to the other when not secured, and are used extensively in press tool construction. Their profile is shown in Fig.91, as is their symbol.

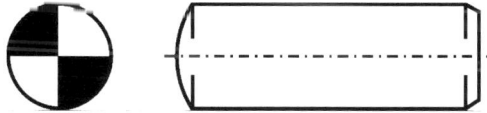

**Fig.91. Dowel Symbol and Profile.**

Dowels are a push fit in both components, see Fig.85, and it should be possible to push the dowel in with the thumb. There is a saying about the fit of dowels:

**"If you use a hammer to drive in a dowel, you will need a heavier hammer to drive it out again."**

The usual fit is H7/j6, but again a tolerance exercise will show whether this is ideal for the work being designed. In any given situation the fit of a silver steel dowel may not be the same as that for a hardened and ground dowel, and both fits may vary according to the materials from which the components are made. If in doubt, a practical trial should be held to determine the best fit before appending to the drawing

## PRECISION ENGINEERING.

Precision engineering requires parts being made to precise dimensions on very accurate CNC machines. The tolerances used for precision Limits and Fits are 0.1 or less of those in general engineering. Working to one tenth of a micron (0.0001mm) is possible under the right circumstances, and this level of accuracy makes a given fit more certain in its performance.

The snag with such precision is that components made to these limits can become temperature sensitive. For example, a precision shaft and bearing are a slide fit when kept in a temperature-controlled room which is set to 20°C. Then the shaft is removed, taken to a room which is at 25°C, and left for an hour.

After that time it is returned to the original room where it will be found that it will not slide through the bearing, the expansion having exceeded the clearance. It will only become a slide fit again when it is the same temperature as the bearing.

Tolerance exercises are essential to guarantee the correct operation of precision bearings in situ.

# CHAPTER 8.

## QUALITY CONTROL AND INTERCHANGEABILITY.

Although some designers start with the details and work their way up to the General Arrangement, experience has shown that this is a risky road to take as it can lead to serious errors and omissions being made. It is advisable to start with the General Arrangement, and this is necessary in industry when working to a national standard, especially the BS 'Kitemark'. In this case, as well as the Drawing Office having a set procedure to follow, a Quality Control department is also necessary to police the company's method of working.

## HOW NOT TO GET A KITEMARK.

One UK company, a maker of special-purpose machines, believed that the acquisition of the BSI 'Kitemark' was highly desirable as with it the firm would be known for the quality of its products, so it applied for BS9001 approval.

However, the company's attitude to design was that it was a necessary evil, and the less money and time spent upon it the better. It was always failing to allow the Drawing Office staff enough time for any new work, so that carefully considered designs which would go together easily and work well right away, often being labelled 'straight from the drawing board', were not possible. Everything was rushed. The company did not allow for the fact, which is almost a law of nature, that **the first design solution is usually the most complex and simpler solutions come later.**

Naturally the firm's often inadequately-considered designs led to many problems during construction as parts did not work as required, so the firm ignored the Drawing Office. It simply altered the part as required in the workshop and installed it. This left the Drawing Office staff unaware of the alteration and the drawing not matching the part fitted to the machine.

The same machine could have as many as twenty such modified parts. As a result, spare parts made to the original drawings would not fit the machine, and the existing, usually defective, parts would have to be copied so the repair could be completed. Permission for the Kitemark was refused as the firm's approach was contrary to the BSI Kitemark requirements.

The Standard insists that every part can be traced from the General Arrangement and if a part is altered then its drawing must be amended and the changes recorded upon it. The issue of the drawing is raised and the old issues kept in the Drawing Office Archive. so that replacement parts can be made from them.

## INTERCHANGEABILITY AND TRACEABILITY.

Interchangeability and traceability are the whole purpose of the BSI Kitemark. Quality Control is often confused with Inspection, which is often a section within the Quality Control Department. Quality Control is not how well the parts are made, which the job of Inspection, but the integrity of the paper system. So in that sense it can be considered a 'paper-chase'.

To hold the Kitemark the firm has to have a Quality Control Procedure. The Drawing Office must be considered an investment, not an expense, and it must be central to that procedure. In firms holding the Kitemark, Quality Control Assessments are frequently performed to ensure that the system is being followed and that the correct issue of the drawing is being used by the shop floor staff. The reason for this is connected with after-sales service.

Here is a diary for one machine part made under the Kitemark.

| | | |
|---|---|---|
| **2 October** | **1974** | Original Issue **'A'** drawing. Part has an M8 hole tapped in it. |
| **March** | **1976** | Tapped hole altered to M10. This change is recorded as **"Issue B 3-3-76. M10 tapped hole was M8."** Issue B placed in the 'Current Drawings' file. Issue **'A'** placed in the Archive file. |
| **September** | **1981** | A replacement request for this part is received. Sales records show the |

| | | |
|---|---|---|
| | | customer's machine was built in 1975. |
| **September** | **1981** | Production Control issues request for the part drawing to the Drawing Office with the date that the machine was sold. The Drawing Office brings out the current drawing which is Issue '**B**' dated 3-3-76. The machine was built before this issue, so it must have used a part made to a previous Issue, and that is Issue 'A' dated 2-10-74. A print of the archived Issue '**A**' drawing accompanies the official order from Production Control to the workshop, which makes the part. |
| **October** | **1981** | Spare part made with M8 hole, and then despatched. Print of Issue A returned to Drawing Office where it is destroyed. |
| **October** | **1981** | Part received by Customer. When checked by the firm's maintenance team it is seen to have an M8 hole which is the correct size, so it will fit without problem. This is the correct procedure. |

The system recommended here will help Drawing Offices run an efficient paper system for all designs, especially where spares are likely to be required. Good filing systems must be acquired for proper records to be kept, and designers employed in these offices must understand the system which is being used and follow its procedures.

## NEW GENERAL ARRANGEMENT DRAWINGS.

Every new General Arrangement (GA) drawing will need breaking down into its constituent parts, as shown in Fig.92.

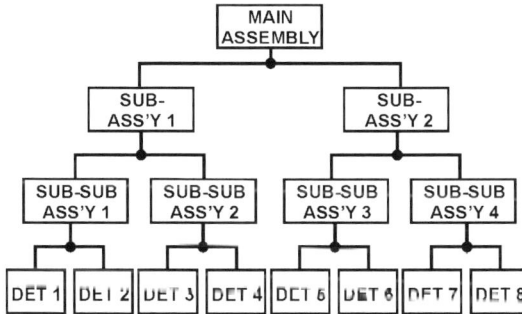

**Fig.92. Typical Analysis of the Parts of a Mechanism.**

The next thing needed is an analysis of the components used in the General Arrangement. Fig.93 gives the Item List for the analysis above.

| Description | Det. No. | Qty. | Mat'l. | Remarks |
|---|---|---|---|---|
| Main Ass'y | 1 | 1 | | Comprises Items 2 &3 |
| Sub Ass'y 1 | 2 | 1 | | Comprises Items 4&5 |
| Sub Ass'y 2 | 3 | 1 | | Comprises Items 6&7 |
| Sub-Sub Ass'y 1 | 4 | 1 | | Comprises Items 8&9 |
| Sub-Sub Ass'y 2 | 5 | 1 | | Comprises Items 10&11 |
| Sub-Sub Ass'y 3 | 6 | 1 | | Comprises Items 12&13 |
| Sub-Sub Ass'y 4 | 7 | 1 | | Comprises Items 14&15 |
| Detail 1 | 8 | 1 | | |
| Detail 2 | 9 | 1 | | |
| Detail 3 | 10 | 1 | | |
| Detail 4 | 11 | 1 | | |
| Detail 5 | 12 | 1 | | |
| Detail 6 | 13 | 1 | | |
| Detail 7 | 14 | 1 | | |
| Detail 8 | 15 | 1 | | |

**Fig.93. Item List for the Mechanism Parts Analysis.**

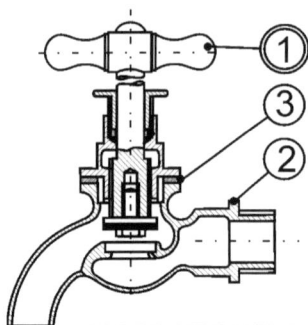

| Description | Det. No. | Qty. | Mat'l. | Remarks |
|---|---|---|---|---|
| Valve Ass'y | 1 | 1 | Fab'd. | See Drg. No. TP4004 |
| Body | 2 | 1 | Brass | Drg. No. TP4002 |
| Washer | 3 | 1 | Fibre | Part 938 |

**Fig.94. Water Tap, or Faucet, with Parts Marked.**

The various components on each assembly drawing are indicated with a number in a circle as shown in the Water Tap, or Faucet, in Fig.94. Sub-Assemblies are shown by double circles. The Item List now has to be written and the individual components identified so that the design of the details can commence, see Fig.95.

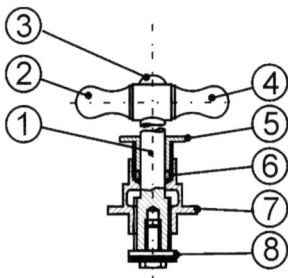

| Description | Det. No. | Qty. | Mat'l. | Remarks |
|---|---|---|---|---|
| Spindle | 1 | 1 | | See Drg. No. TP4004 |
| Handle | 2 | 1 | | See Drg. No. TP4005 |
| Rd. Hd. Screw | 3 | 1 | Steel | Part 453 |
| Gland | 4 | 1 | | See Drg. No.TP4006 |
| Packing | 5 | 1 | | See Drg. No.TP4007 |
| Body | 6 | 1 | Cotton | Part 822 |
| Washer Ass'y. | 7 | 1 | | See Drg. No.TP4008 |
| Hex.Hd.Screw | 8 | 1 | Brass | Part 455 |

**Fig.95. Item List for Water Tap, or Faucet, Parts.**

In Fig.92 the reference in Detail 1 of the List is to another drawing which shows the valve assembled. This is called a Sub-Assembly. It means that the valve is assembled on one production line in accordance with its Assembly Drawing and Item List, and the completed sub-assembly is then transferred to another line where the product is assembled in accordance with Figs.9 and 10.

As this example shows, the Item List will need to reflect the way the assembly will be built on the production line, although in most cases it will be obvious.

# CHAPTER 9.

## ANSWERS TO C' SERIES EXERCISES.

**EXERCISE C1.**

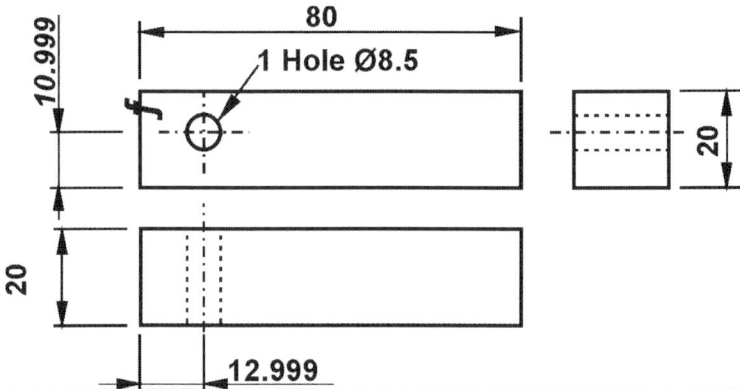

**Fig.96. Block with One Hole, Worst Case Scenario.**

In Fig.96 the two linear dimensions have extended by 0.999 and the hole has increased in diameter by the same amount. This part will pass inspection because all the dimensions are within their respective tolerances. Technically, this part has no cumulative or non-cumulative dimensions but has been included as it leads to Figs.96 and 97.

**EXERCISE C2.**

What can possibly go wrong with two holes in a block? In the Scenario shown in Fig.97 the Worst Case has become real.

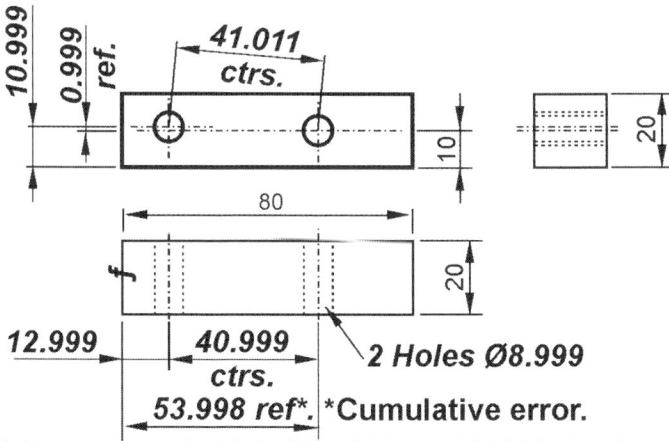

**Fig.97. Block with Two Holes, Worst Case Scenario.**

The block would have been acceptable if the left hand hole had not moved upwards. This is an unexpected movement which has stretched the centre distance beyond the tolerance, and so the block will fail inspection.


## EXERCISE C3

Now a third hole is added to the block, but this runs at right angles to the other two holes, and is dimensioned from the right hand end.

**This type of error is typical when datums and dimensioning are not understood. There are special circumstances on long parts, like beams, where two datums are necessary, but this in not one of them.**


It can be seen in Fig.98, where the two left hand holes have moved to the right, but the right hand hole has moved to the left from its different datum. The contrary flow has put the right hand hole on a collision course with the middle hole. The result is that the centre distance reduces to 7.003, causing an interference of 0.997 and resulting in the part being scrap. There are exceptions to the single datum rule, and an example is given in Fig.

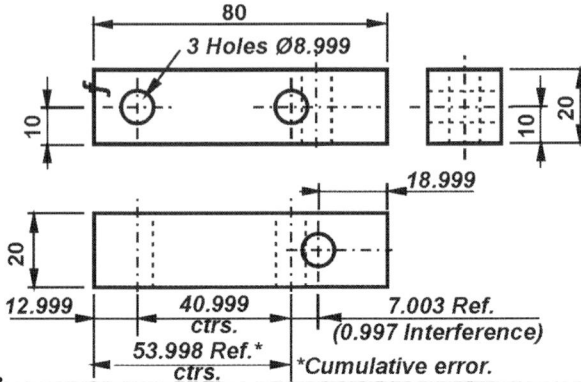

**Fig.98. Block with Three Holes, Worst Case Scenario.**

**EXERCISE C4.**

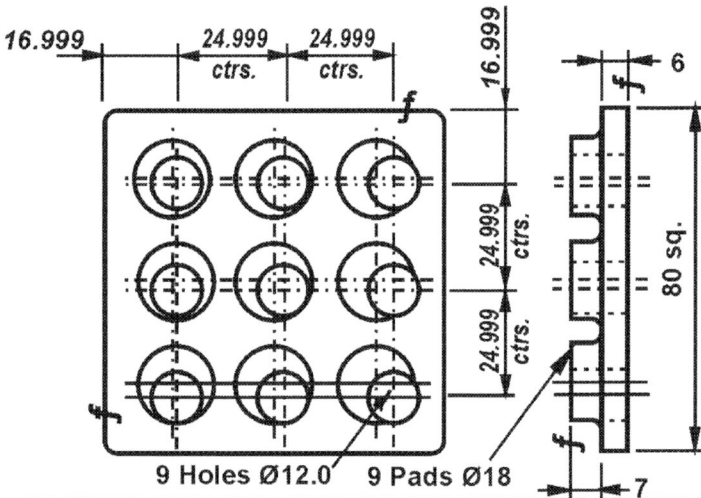

**Fig.99. Cast Iron Plate, Worst Case Scenario.**

In Fig.99 all the centre distances have expanded to 24.999 and the holes have moved diagonally downwards to the right. There is a progressive worsening of the situation as the cumulative dimensions flow away from the datums. This puts most of the holes outside the pads, and clearly this is not acceptable. This situation is called **'The Movement of Holes'**. It is something every designer needs to monitor when components carry cumulative dimensions. There are several ways to overcome this problem but that is when the designer's ingenuity comes into play. In this case proposed larger pads have been drawn, see Fig.100. This shows the same situation as in Fig.99 but since it has the larger pads the finished component may now be acceptable.

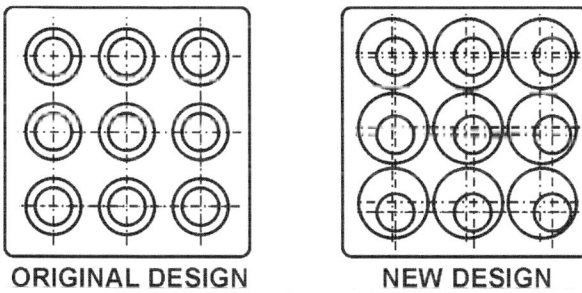

ORIGINAL DESIGN        NEW DESIGN

**Fig.100. Cast Iron Plate, New Design.**

It should now be seen how useful this tool is for discovering possible design problems and allowing corrective action to be taken before the drawing is issued.

**EXERCISE C5.**

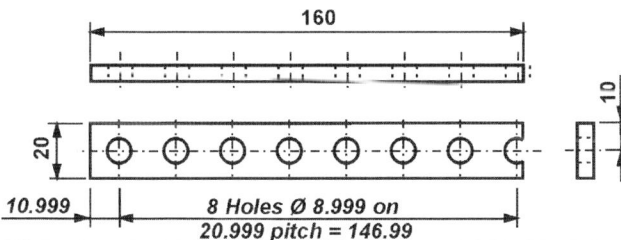

160

10

20

10.999

8 Holes Ø 8.999 on
20.999 pitch = 146.99

**Fig.101. Drilled Strip, Worst Case Scenario.**

Fig.108 shows that the strip is scrap, but it would have passed if there had been more metal at the right hand end.

**EXERCISE C6.**

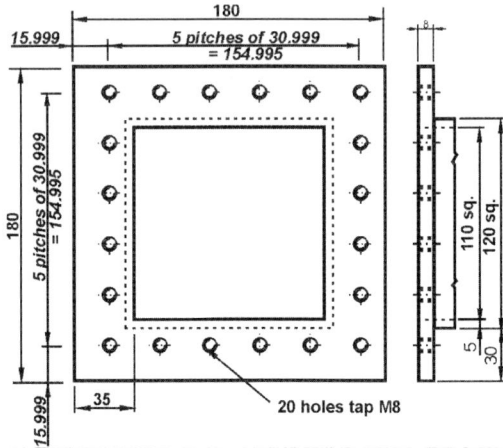

**Fig. 102. Ventilation Duct Flange, Worst Case Scenario.**

There is nothing wrong in Fig.102, so it will pass inspection.

**EXERCISE C7.**

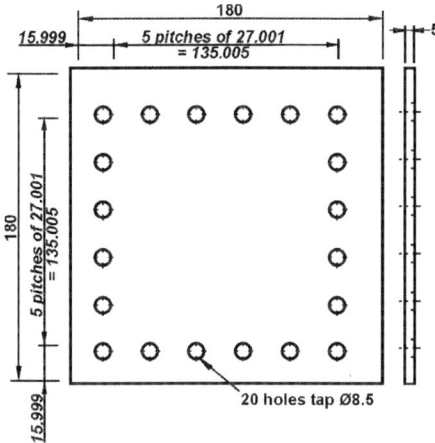

**Fig. 103. Duct Flange Blanking Plate, Worst Case Scenario.**

Again there is nothing wrong with the finished component in Fig.103, so it will pass inspection. **Will C6 and C7 fit together?** Despite both passing inspection they will not match, see Fig.104.

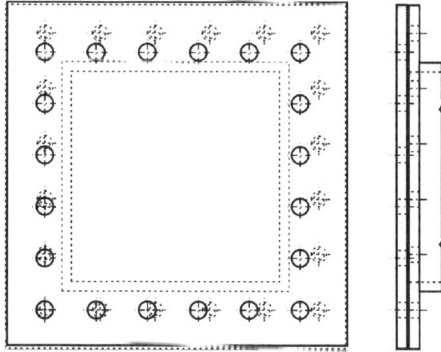

**Fig.104. Duct Flange and Flange Plate.**

This sometimes happens when items made by one firm have to fit parts made by another. It is known as an 'Interface' problem and should be resolved before manufacturing starts. In 1858 an attempt was made to run a telephone cable across the Atlantic ocean from the UK to the USA.

One half of the cable was made in Britain, the other in America. The cable-laying ships each set sail laying half of the cable, and they met at the agreed spot. The cable-layers then tried to connect the two half cables together, only to find the connections were mismatched.

As they tightened one end it slackened the other end.

The cable-layers bodged a joint which allowed a few weak signals to be transmitted for a few weeks, but it soon failed and the £500,000 invested was lost because they had not agreed the interface beforehand.

## EXERCISE C8.

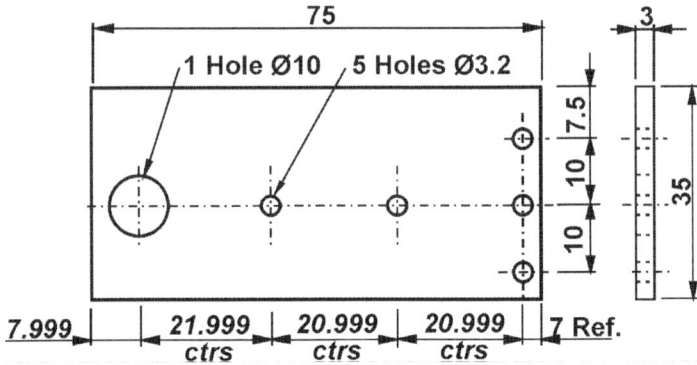

**Fig.105. Small Plate, Worked from Datum.**

The component is satisfactory, as shown in Fig.105, and would pass inspection.

## EXERCISE C9.

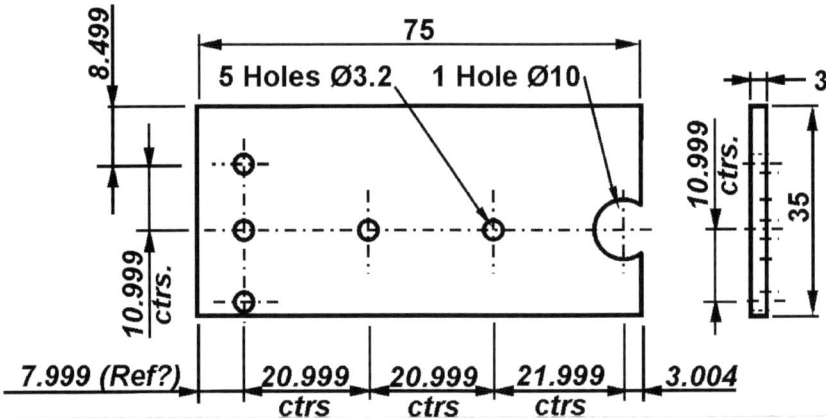

**Fig.106. Small Plate Worked from Reference dimension.**

In Fig.106 the large hole has moved to such an extent that it is halfway out of the plate and would be rejected by inspection. Can it happen? Definitely.

It is a similar outcome to that of a large real tool designed by the author but incorrectly drilled in the tool room of a large domestic appliance manufacturer in the late 1960's, when the jig borer started at the Reference dimension instead of at the Datum hole. The Tool Room Superintendent tried to say that the drawing was wrong, until the designer pointed out that the datum hole was marked as such.

## EXERCISE C10.

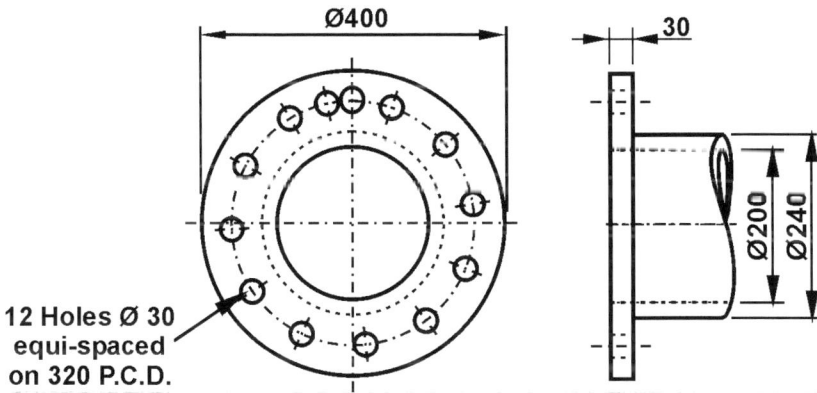

**Fig.107. Pipe Flange, Worst Case Scenario.**

It will be seen in Fig.107 that all the holes are progressively further out of position, and it would clearly fail inspection.

# CHAPTER 10.

## ANSWERS TO 'N' SERIES EXERCISES.

**EXERCISE N1.**

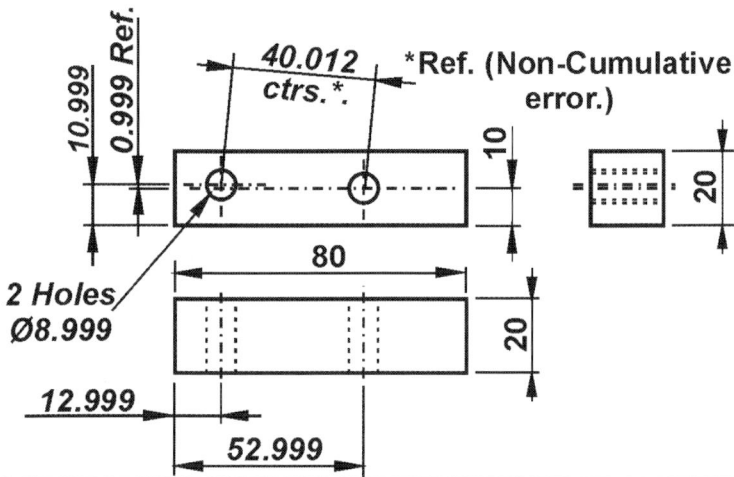

**Fig.108. Block with Two Holes.**

In Fig.108 the Reference dimension is simply a check to prove that the effective centre distance, which has been added for comparison with Exercise C1, is within the tolerance so it will pass inspection.

**EXERCISE N2.**

In Fig.109 all the holes have been dimensioned from the left hand datum. The left hand two holes moved to the right, and the right hand hole maintained its clearance even though it did not move. So it would pass inspection.

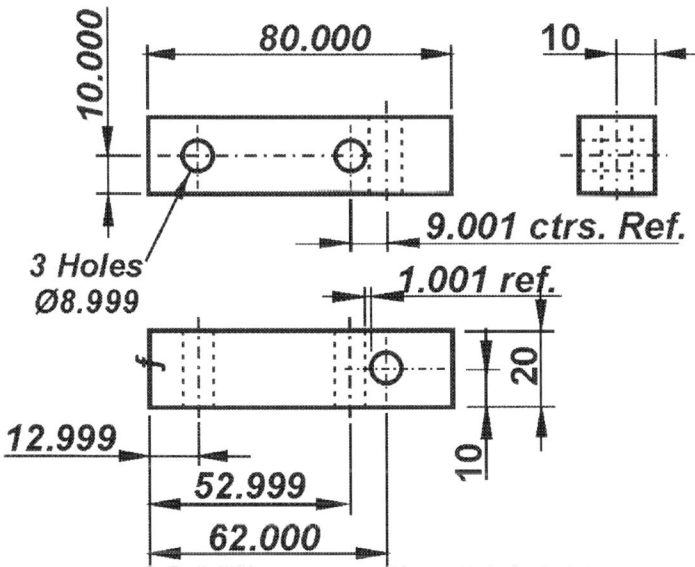

**Fig.109. Block with Three Holes.**

**EXERCISE N3.**

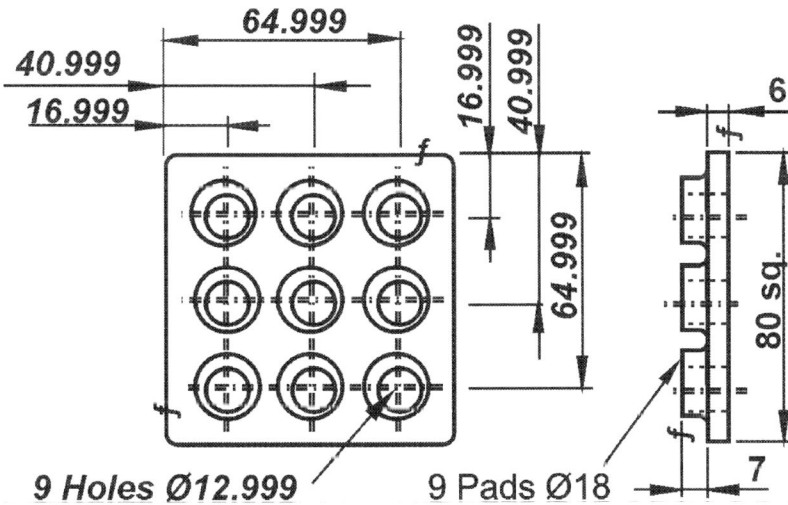

**Fig.110. Cast Iron Plate.**

Fig.110 would pass inspection.

# EXERCISE N4.

The result is satisfactory in Fig.111.

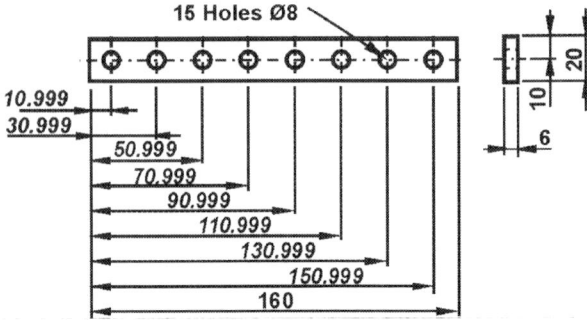

**Fig.111. Drilled Strip.**

# EXERCISE N5.

Fig.112 is perfectly satisfactory and would pass inspection.

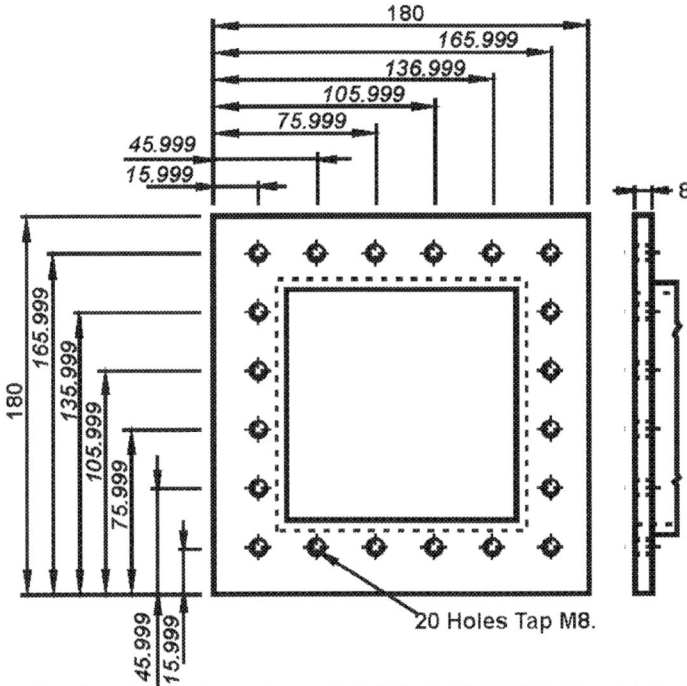

**Fig. 112. Ventilation Duct Flange.**

## EXERCISE N6.

Fig.113, too, is satisfactory and would pass inspection.

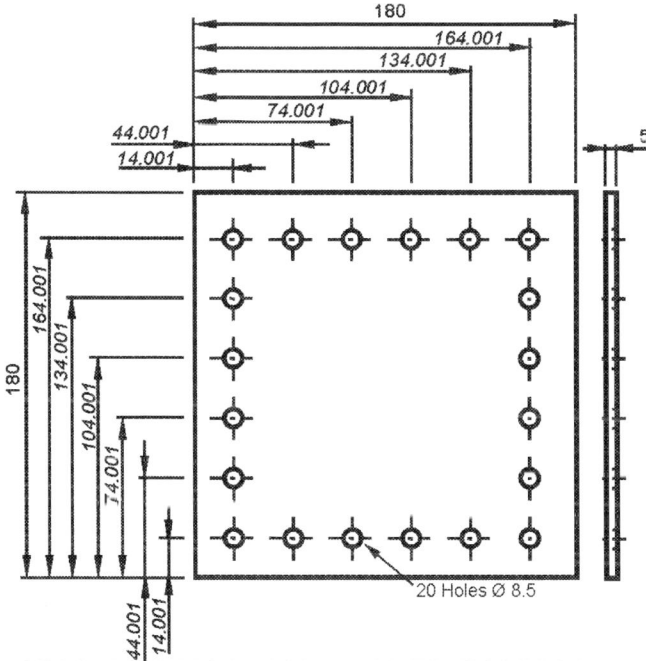

**Fig.113. Duct Flange Blanking Plate.**

Fig.114 shows they will fit together.

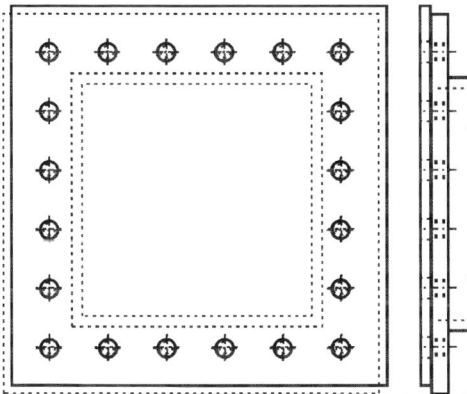

**Fig.114. The Duct Flange and Blanking Plate.**

## EXERCISE N8.

The plate in Fig.115 is satisfactory and would pass inspection.

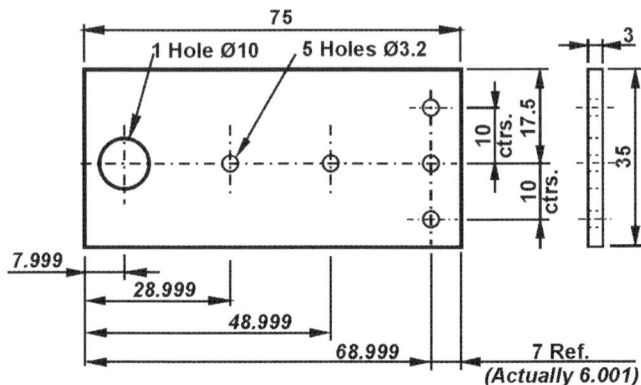

**Fig.115. Small Plate, Worked from Datum.**

## EXERCISE N9.

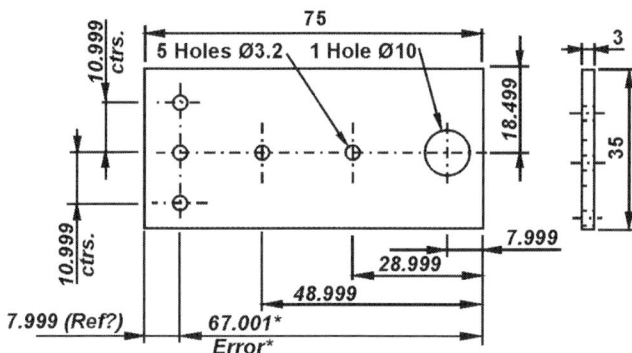

**Fig.116. Small Plate, Worked from Reference Dimension.**

In Fig.116 all the holes have moved towards the Datum by 0.999. The centre of the large hole is now 6.001 from the end of the plate. That leaves only 1mm wall thickness on the centre line. Technically it is still within the drawing tolerance, but whether it will pass inspection is debatable. If more metal can be left around the holes it could prevent wastage. This example indicates how a designer can protect his design even if it is made incorrectly.

**EXERCISE N10.**

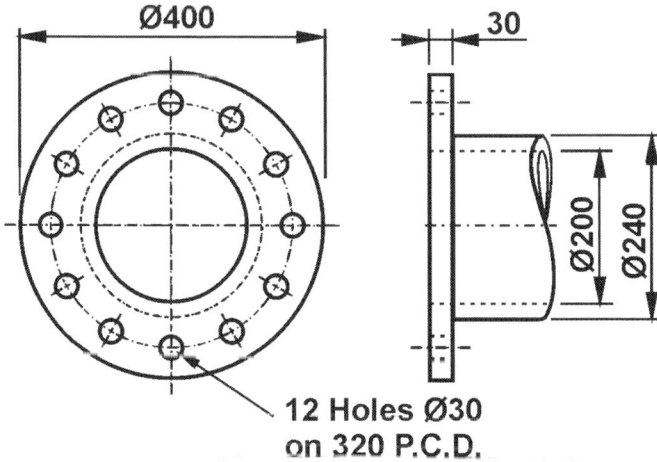

**Fig.117. Pipe Flange.**

In Fig.117 the top hole is slightly elongated, but not enough to be noticeable. To overcome this, the holes are often drilled with pilot holes, and then opened to size afterwards. It should pass inspection either way.

# CHAPTER 11.

## ANSWERS TO 'P' SERIES EXERCISES.

**EXERCISE P1.**

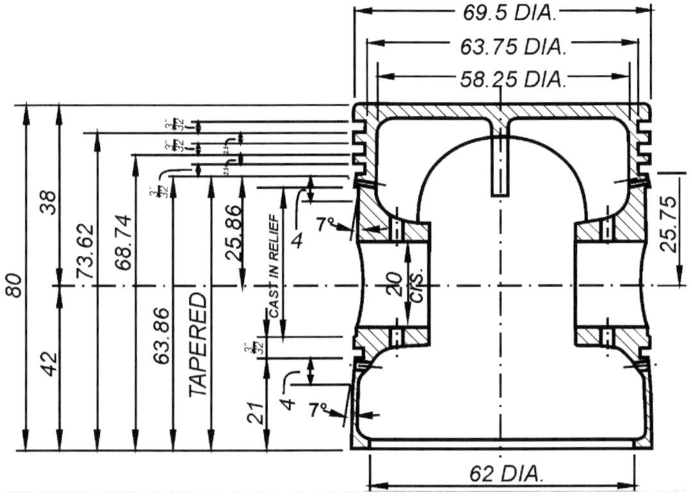

**Fig.118. Piston.**

Fig.118 Errors:

1. Numbers let into dimension lines, top right.

2. Double dimensioning: 80, 38 and 42 dimensions.

3. Double dimensioning: 73.62, 3/32", and 4 dimensions.

4. Double dimensioning: 68.74 and multiple dimensions above it.

5. Imperial dimensions on a metric drawing.

6. Bottom groove has two dim'ns to centre line: 25.86 and 25.75.

7. Multiple indirect dimensions.

8. Double dimensioning by subtraction. 38 = 80 - 42.

9. Double dimensioning by subtraction. 38 = 63.86 - 25.86.

10. Double dimensioning by subtraction. 38 = 63.86 + (incorrectly)

a. 27.75.

11. Dimension on part: 20. Diameter sign omitted.

**Total = 11.**

*This example was based upon a drawing in an Engineering Workshop Drawing book that was used by Technical Colleges.*

**EXERCISE P2.**

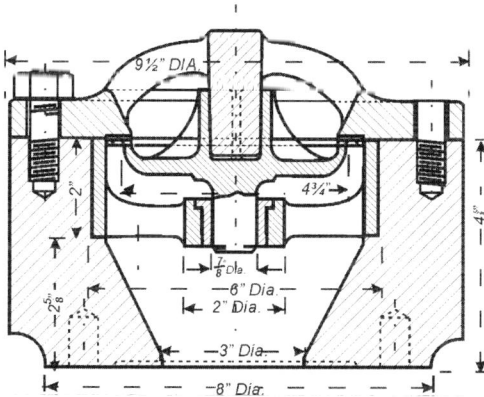

**Fig.119. L.N.E.R. Anti-Vacuum Valve.**

Fig.119 Errors:

1. Dimension let into dimension line.

2. Bad arrowheads and lines.

3. Double dimensioning. 4-5/8" = 2-5/8" + 2".

4. Dimensions on hatching.

5. Dimension on component.

6. Badly placed dimension on component.

7. Confusion of dimensions in centre cavity.

8. Relief at bottom shown hidden but should have been shown in section.

**Total = 8.**

*This was originally published in a full-size-railway magazine, and reprinted in a book on the design of full-size steam locomotives.*

**EXERCISE P3.**

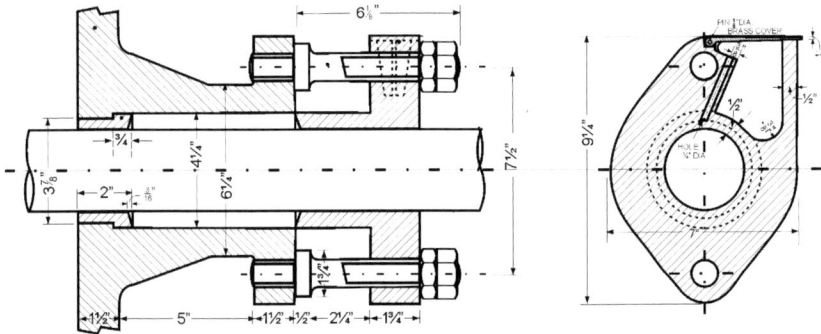

**Fig.120. Horizontal Stuffing Box.**

Fig.120 Errors:

1. Dimension let into dimension line.

2. Dimension on hatching.

3. Radii on end elevation not given.

4. Details of lid assembly vague.

5. Stud dimensioned except for thread size.

6. Clearance hole for stud not shown in gland.

7. Bush detailed on the assembly.

**Total = 7.**

*This example was based upon a drawing in the same Engineering Workshop Drawing book that was used by Technical Colleges.*

112

## EXERCISE P4.

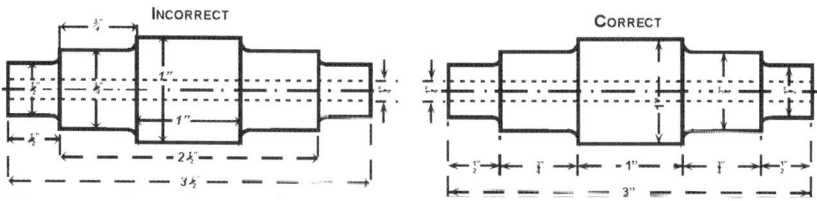

## Fig.121. Stepped Shaft.

Despite the labels 'Correct' and 'Incorrect' both drawings are incorrect.

Double dimensioning is shown as an arithmetic sum.

Fig.121 Errors:

1. Numbers inserted in dimension lines.

2. Bad dimension and projection lines and arrowheads.

3. Crossed dimensions written on component.

4. Irrationally placed dimension (top right of right hand shaft.

5. Upright sizes on vertical dimensions.

6. Double Dimensions. $3\frac{1}{2}” = \frac{1}{2}” + \frac{3}{4}” + 1” + \frac{3}{4}” + \frac{1}{2}”$.

7. Fractions placed correct way but poor location on centre line of left hand shaft.

8. Two diameters omitted. **It should not be assumed that they are the same as on the other side of the shaft.**

9. No mention of fillet radii.

**Total = 9.**

*This presentation was taken from a drawing included in the same Workshop Drawing book used by Technical Colleges.*

## EXERCISE P5.

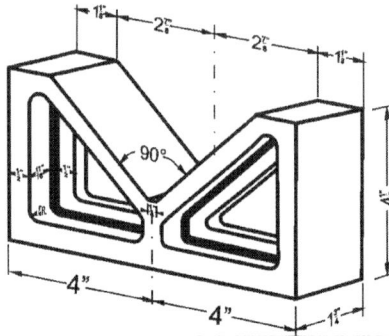

**Fig.122. 'V' Block.**

Fig.122 Errors:

1. Dimensioning an Isometric View. Apart from that, the other errors are:

2. Dimensions let into dimension lines.

3. Double dimensions, all top and all bottom.

4. Double dimensions, top and bottom left.

5. Double dimensions, top and bottom right.

6. Dimensioning to start of radius. Dimensioning is done to the point of origin of the radius.

7. Dimension for flat in centre not shown clearly or if it is central.

8. No direct dimension is given for the height or length of the 45° face. It would have been better to have given the length or height of the slope and left the flat without a dimension or as a reference size.

**Total = 8.**

*This example was taken from a drawing issued by Joint County Technical Colleges.*

## EXERCISE P6.

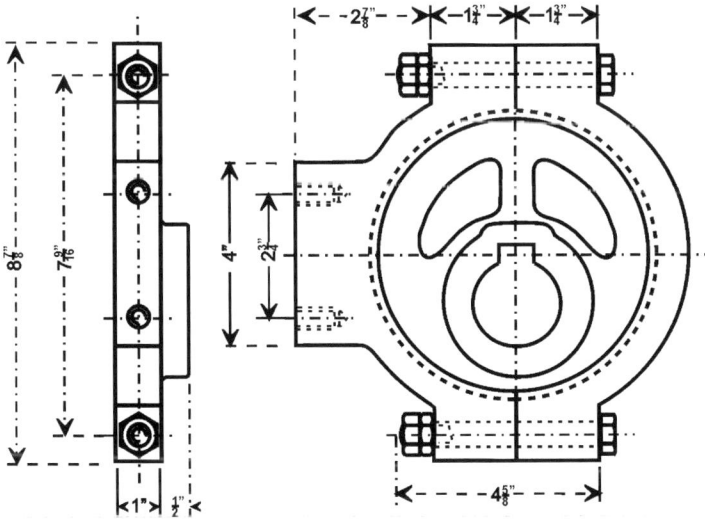

**Fig.123. Eccentric Sheave and Strap.**

Fig.123 Errors:

1.  Numbers inserted in dimension lines.

2.  Bad dimension and projection lines and arrowheads.

3.  Thread of tapped hole not stated

4.  ½" dimension is vague. Is it for the stud or the hole?

5.  7/8" dimension has arrowhead but no dimension line.

6.  The eccentric diameter given indirectly. It is $2 \times (2"$ rad. $+ 7/8")$.

7.  Confusion of dimensions around eccentric shaft hole.

8.  Depth of tapped holes not stated.

9.  Dimension to line of studs in elevation not given.

10. Keyway width given but not depth.

   **Total =10.**

*This presentation was taken from a drawing included in the same Workshop Drawing book that was used by Technical Colleges.*

**EXERCISE P7.**

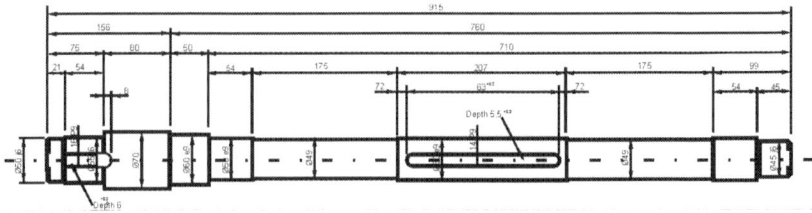

**Fig.124. Machine Shaft.**

Fig.124 must be the supreme example of a lack of understanding of dimensions and tolerances. The impression given is that the person who drew it intended the length of 915 to be incontrovertible.

The double dimensions are given as a set of sums, and it is suggested that these be studied on the drawing. By following each entry below the errors will be seen.

Errors:

1. Double Dimensioning. $915 = 760 + 155$.

2. Double Dimensioning. $915 = 760 + 80 + 75$.

3. Double Dimensioning. $915 = 760 + 80 + 54 + 21$.

4. Double Dimensioning. $915 = 710 + 50 + 155$.

5. Double Dimensioning. $915 = 710 + 80 + 75$.

6. Double Dimensioning. $915 = 710 + 80 + 54 + 21$.

7. Double Dimensioning. $760 = 710 + 50$.

8. Double Dimensioning. $710 = 99 + 175 + 207 + 175 + 54$.

9. Double Dimensioning. $710 = 99 + 175 + 72 + 63 + 72 + 175 + 54$.

10. Double Dimensioning. $710 = 45 + 55 + 175 + 207 + 175 + 54$.

11. Double Dimensioning. $710 = 45 + 55 + 175 + 72 + 63 + 72 + 175 + 54$.

12. Double Dimensioning.  99 = 45 + 54.

13. Double Dimensioning.  207 = 72 + 63 +72.

14. Double Dimensioning.  156 = 80 + 75.

15. Double Dimensioning.  156 = 80 + 54 +21.

16. Double Dimensioning.  75 = 54 + 21.

17. Keyway is out of scale.

18. Keyway dimension to the centre line has been omitted.

19. Some diameters not clear.

20. Indirect slot dimensions.

21. Radii at ends of slots not mentioned.

22. Dimensions for end chamfers not stated.

**Total = 22.**

*This example was based upon a Turkish drawing published on the Internet.*

# CHAPTER 12.

## REWORKING THE PRESENTATIONS.

The items given in the presentations shown in Chapter 5 were reasonably well drawn in outline, with one or two exceptions, but were ruined by haphazard and illogical dimensioning that lacked clarity and caused confusion. The same items have been reworked to show the student how they should have been done.

## P1. PISTON.

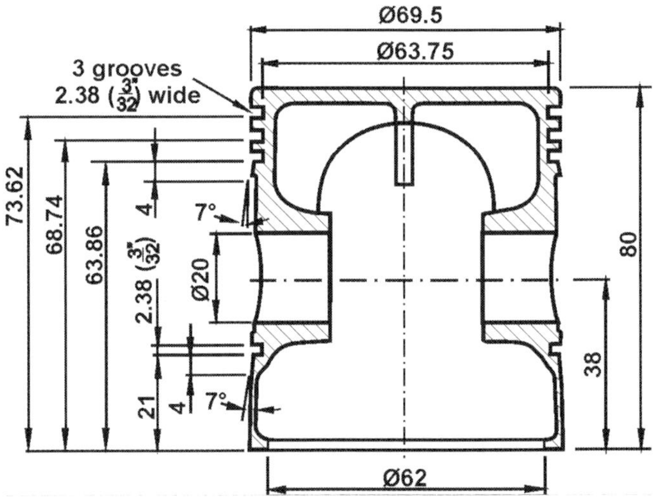

**Fig.125. Piston (Revised).**

Notice how few dimensions are really needed in Fig.125. The heights have been placed on the right hand side, leaving the left hand side for the groove dimensions.

To save the complexity of dimensioning every groove, a block dimension has been given for the top three grooves, but the bottom groove is a separate item and has its own dimensions. With this arrangement a turner would have no trouble machining the piston blank.

Note that the upper inside diameter has been omitted, as it is a casting dimension and is not needed on a machining drawing. The lower Ø62 diameter is necessary as it is a machining dimension.

## P2. L.N.E.R. ANTI-VACUUM VALVE.

Fig.126 shows an assembly where all the components have been ballooned and an Item List placed below. All the necessary information is contained in this list, and it would also give the detail drawing numbers.

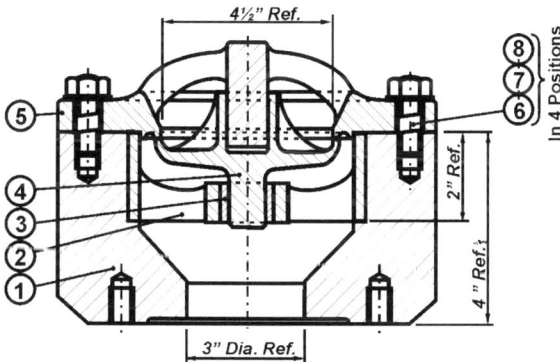

| Description | Det. No. | Qty. | Mat'l. | Remarks |
|---|---|---|---|---|
| Washer, Plain | 8 | 4 | Steel | |
| Hex. Nut, Full | 7 | 4 | Steel | |
| Stud | 6 | 4 | Steel | |
| Retainer Guide | 5 | 1 | Brass | |
| Valve | 4 | 1 | Brass | |
| Bush, Plain | 3 | 1 | Bronze | Pressed into Det.2 |
| Spider | 2 | 1 | Brass | |
| Body | 1 | 1 | Brass | |

**Fig.126. L.N.E.R. Anti-Vacuum Valve (Revised).**

## P3. Horizontal Stuffing Box.

Fig.127 is another assembly which has been given the same treatment as the Valve above. The only difference is that the Gland is a Sub-Assembly, and will have its own assembly drawing and set of detail drawings. The Box itself should have a casting drawing and a machining drawing.

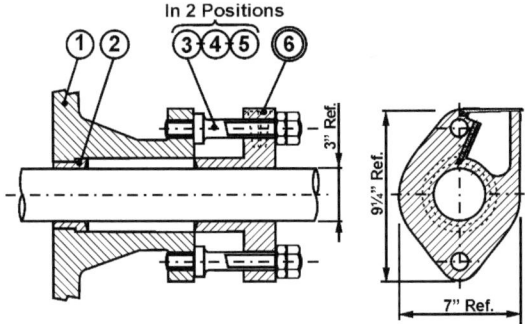

| Description | Det. No. | Qty. | Mat'l. | Remarks |
|---|---|---|---|---|
| Gland Assembly | 6 | 1 | Fab'd. | See Drg. No. |
| Hex. Nut, Full | 5 | 1 | M.S. | |
| Hex. Locknut | 4 | 1 | M.S. | |
| Stud | 3 | 1 | M.S. | |
| Bush, headed | 2 | 1 | Bronze | |
| Body | 1 | 1 | C.I. | |

**Fig.127. Horizontal Stuffing Box (Revised).**

## P4. STEPPED SHAFT.

Only one drawing is needed, as shown in Fig.128, and in it all left hand side diameters have been logically arranged together at the left hand end, and the right hand side diameters at the right hand side. It would normally be assumed that all the diameters are concentric, but a note to this effect on, or the concentric symbol added to, the drawing would not go amiss.

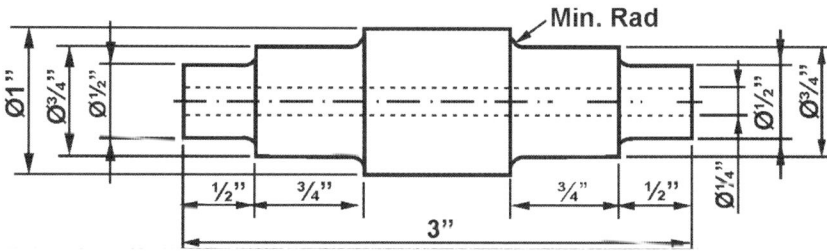

## Fig.128. Stepped Shaft (Revised).

The original drawing omitted to say what two diameters were, forcing the operator to make assumptions. This is not a wise thing to do, as the wrong assumption leading to a failed component will result in blame being laid at the drawing creator's doorstep. It is always safe to dimension all diameters. **The designer should never allow the workshop to interpret his meaning – it should be crystal-clear.**

The radii are covered with a global statement, as the exact radius is unimportant and is usually governed by the tip of the tool being used. The centre section does not have a dimension for its length unless it is necessary for correct functioning, as it would be for a railway wagon axle when it will be the 'back-to-back' dimension for the track gauge. The overall length then should be a reference dimension to avoid double dimensioning.

NB. For practical purposes when making the shaft, if Bright Mild Steel round bar is used then the outside should be skimmed true in the lathe before turning the steps. The rule is:

**If mild steel is not ground, it is not round.**

If necessary a note on the drawing can be added about this extra operation.

## P5. 'V' BLOCK.

It is bad practice to dimension an isometric view, as shown in Fig.129. It should have a casting drawing as well as a machining drawing.

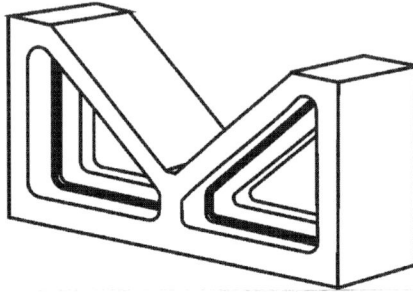

**Fig.129. 'V' Block (Revised).**

## P6. ECCENTRIC SHEAVE AND STRAP.

In Fig.130 is yet another assembly which has been ballooned and an Item List issued.

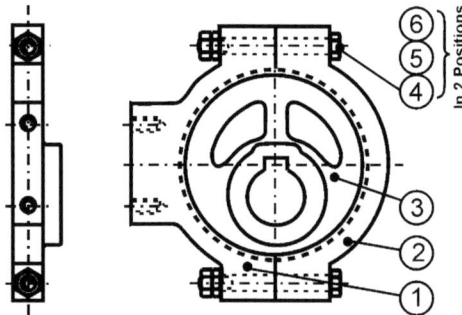

| Description | Det. No. | Qty. | Mat'l. | Remarks |
|---|---|---|---|---|
| Hex. Locknut | 6 | 2 | Steel | |
| Hex. Nut, Full | 5 | 2 | Steel | |
| Hex. Hd. Bolt | 4 | 2 | Steel | |
| Sheave | 3 | 1 | M.S. | |
| Strap Strap | 2 | 1 | Bronze | |
| Strap Body | 1 | 1 | Bronze | |

**Fig.130. Eccentric Sheave and Strap (Revised).**

## P7. MACHINE SHAFT.

In Fig.131 the shaft has been re-dimensioned, the keyway corrected in length, and the relationship of the keyway to the centre line added.

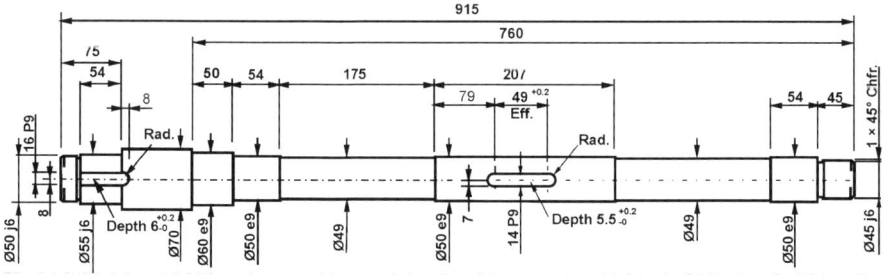

**Fig.131. Machine Shaft (Revised).**

# CHAPTER 13.

## THE DONKEY SYNDROME.

There are two Standard Rules for datums:

**1. All dimensions flow from a single datum, usually on the left or at the bottom.**

**2. One datum should abut another datum. The reason for this is that it is pointless to put the flat face of a datum against one that is not flat.** If a sump casting does not have its top flange machined flat, it will not give an oil-tight seal when fastened to the machined flange at the bottom of the engine.

The name given to the lack of understanding of Rule 2 by the author is **'The Donkey Syndrome',** and anyone suffering from it is a Donkey.

So what is the Donkey Syndrome?

A. The inability to recognize an exception to Rule 1, and insist that the component must conform to this rule.

B. The inability to know that Rule 2 takes precedence over Rule 1.

C. The stubborn refusal to accept his own inabilities given in A and B, so proving technical ignorance.

Fig.132 shows a set of components being made under the supervision of a Donkey.

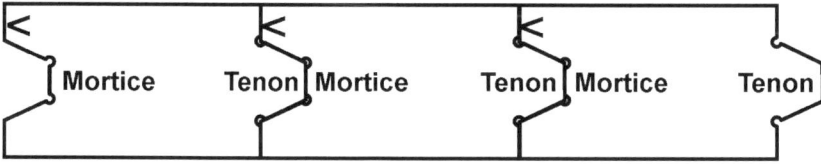

**Fig.132. Set of Tiles.**

As Rule 2 applies here it is clear that the mating faces must both be datums, as in Fig.133.

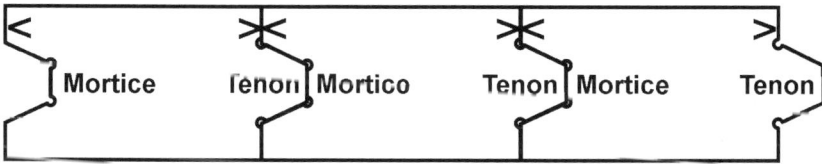

**Fig.133. Tiles with Mating Faces Shown as Datums.**

It is now quite clear that each of these tiles has two axial datums, and the designer realized that the plate was an exception to Rule 1 and dimensioned it in accordance with Rule 2, as shown in Fig.134.

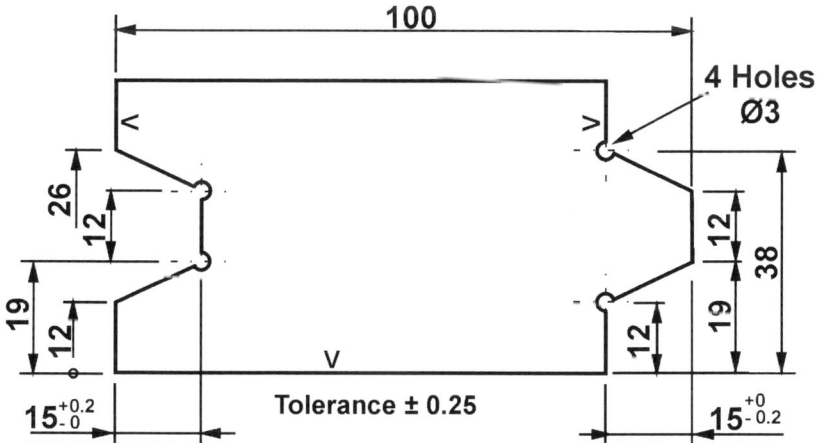

**Fig134. Tile Dimensions.**

It was unfortunate for the poor fitter making this part that his overseer was a Donkey, who said that the drawing was wrong. He brayed that there should only be one datum, and that was on the left. He insisted that the fitter made it to the his dimension of '85' which he added to the drawing, as shown in Fig.135.

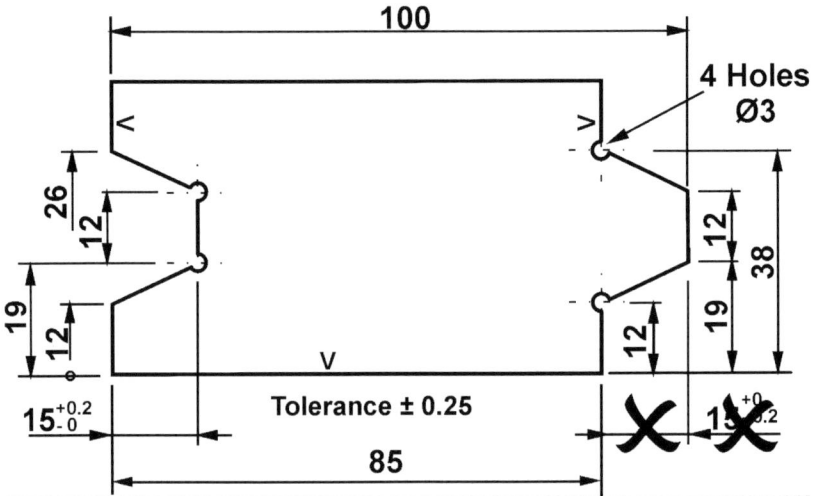

**Fig.135. Tile with the 'Donkey' Dimension.**

However, the Donkey had unwisely strayed out of the pasture of 'The Arrogance of Technical Ignorance.' Altering a drawing without permission from the issuing authority is breaking the copyright and against copyright law. If the drawing is wrong the fact should be reported to the Drawing Office and it will make the necessary changes. If it finds out about the unauthorized alteration it will report the fact to the appropriate authority and the offender person will be disciplined.

As much of the dimensioning is not relevant to the Donkey Dimension, Fig.136 will only show the axial dimensions.

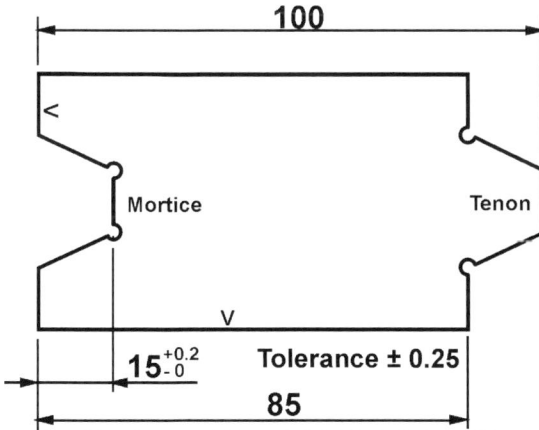

**Fig.136. Tile with Minimal Dimensions.**

## Worse Case Scenario

This will need to be considered for Fig.136. There are only three dimensions involved. The worst case will be the overall length rising to **100.25**, the mortice staying at **15.00**, and the Donkey Dimension dropping to **69.75**. Therefore the tenon length will be **100.25 – (84.75) = 15.50.**

But the drawing states the tenon tolerance to be 15 +0/-0.2, so using the Donkey dimension not only defies the drawing tolerance, it risks making the tenon go beyond the tolerance and too long to fit the mortice as intended, resulting in the datum faces not touching,

That is what the Worst Case Scenario has shown. So what did the Donkey Dimension reveal about the supervisor?

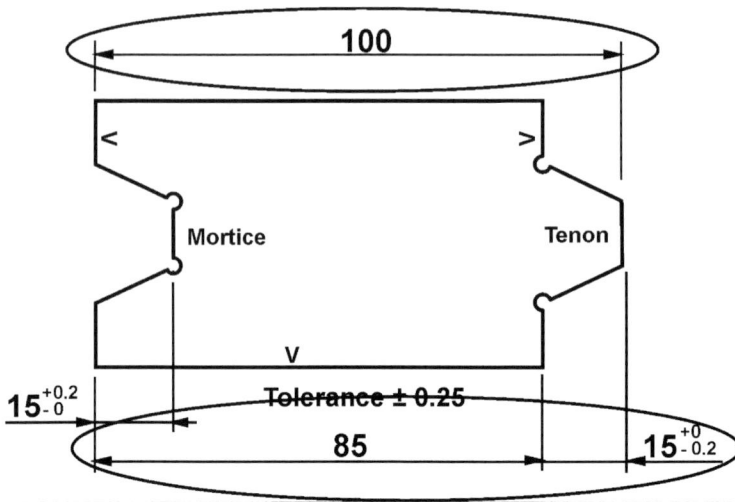

**Fig.137. Tile with All Axial Dimensions.**

Fig.137 shows his unauthorised addition to the drawing. It is a classic example of Double Dimensioning, and the sign of technical ignorance! When the Donkey insisted on the fitter working to the 85 dimension, the fitter told him that it would make the tenon too long. The Donkey would not accept that, as he was as stubborn as only donkeys can be, but the subsequent argument resulted in him being dismissed for misconduct.

As was said inFig.30, one dimension will need discarding, so the essential ones will need determining.

A. The overall length is important.

B. The mortice length is important as it needs to be tightly controlled with a plus tolerance so it will tend to be deeper than nominal.

C. The tenon length is important as it needs to be tightly controlled with a plus tolerance so it will tend to be shorter than nominal

B and C are necessary to ensure that the datum faces will meet.

D. The only dimension left is the Donkey dimension, and it serves no useful purpose. The mortice and tenon are controlled by their requirement to fit together, and the exact distance between them is unimportant, the overall length seeing to that. That is why the Donkey Dimension was omitted in the original design.

**All work that abuts other work at both ends, like the tile, must have datums at both ends.**

# CONCLUSION.

Dimensions are like a two-edged sword. THE TRAINED DESIGNER knows how to use them so he will get the result he requires. THE UNTRAINED DESIGNER thinks that they will do what he wants, but often finds that they don't.

**Always check to see that they will do what you intend them to do by using Worse Case Scenarios, and don't given them any cause to run riot.**

The art of presentation is in obtaining the maximum clarity of the finished drawing. Think about the placement of dimensions at the beginning and avoid crowding them together. If the rules given here are followed, the drawing will be clear and unambiguous. Compare Figs 125 and 131 with the originals in Figs.75 and 81.

There are three old Drawing Office sayings:

- **10% more thought gives a 90% better outcome.**

- **The first design thought of is usually the most complex.**

- **If you want simplicity, add lightness.**

The last one may seem odd, but it is true. If one component can be made to do two jobs the amount of material needed will be less, thus lightening the overall weight, and the assembly will be simpler and more elegant.

It is suggested that the student adopt a 'Self-Assessment' of his/her finished drawing, mentally marking it out of 10. The assessment can also be called a 'Happiness' factor. How happy is the student with the result? Less than 5 means an attempt should be made to improve it, or else redraw it.

An assessment between 6 and 8 is subject to whether there is enough time to improve the drawing, and how best to do it. Between 8 and 9½ it will almost certainly be acceptable, but 10 is perfection. It is always the goal to reach, but it is impossible to get. And there comes a time when the amount of time taken to improve it even by a fraction is outweighed by the cost.

Nevertheless, even with assessments above 8, ways should be considered for improving the next drawing task's assessment, as perfection should be sought even though it is not attainable. However, it is important to know **'when to get off the carousel'**, i.e. when further work will produce little improvement, and that is a situation known as 'The Law of Diminishing Returns'.

One way of reassessing the work is to put the drawing away and leave it for a fortnight. When it is brought out and examined again it is almost certain that something not quite right will become evident and that it can be improved, and any errors that have been made can be corrected.

There is a psychological reason for this procedure. After working intensively on a drawing over a period its creator becomes blind to its defects. Looking at it later means that the blind spot has disappeared and its faults will become apparent. This is why, immediately after finishing a drawing, it is always better to let someone else check it for accuracy.

# APPENDIX.

# TABLE OF IMPERIAL LIMITS AND FITS UP TO 7".

| NOMINAL SIZES | HOLES | SHAFTS | | | | | |
|---|---|---|---|---|---|---|---|
| | BASIC HOLE | INTERFERENCE | | TRANS-ITION | CLEARANCE | | |
| | | u6 | p6 | j6 | h6 | g6 | f7 |
| OVER - UP TO & INCLUDING | H7 | SHRINK | LIGHT PRESS | PUSH | SLIDE | CLOSE RUN | RUN |
| .04 - .12 | +.0004 / +.0 | +.00095 / +.0007 | +.00065 / +.0004 | +.00015 / +.0001 | +.0 / -.00025 | -.0001 / -.00035 | -.0003 / -.0007 |
| .12 - .24 | +.0005 / +.0 | +.00012 / +.0009 | +.0008 / +.0005 | +.0002 / +.0001 | +.0 / -.0003 | -.00015 / -.00045 | -.0004 / -.0009 |
| .24 - .4 | +.0006 / +.0 | +.0016 / +.0012 | +.001 / +.0006 | +.0003 / +.0001 | +.0 / -.0004 | -.0002 / -.0006 | -.0005 / -.0011 |
| .4 - .71 | +.0007 / +.0 | +.0018 / +.0014 | +.0011 / +.0007 | +.0003 / +.0001 | +.0 / -.0004 | -.00025 / -.00065 | -.0006 / -.0013 |
| .71 - .95 | +.0008 / +.0 | +.0021 / +.0016 | +.0013 / +.0008 | +.0003 / +.0002 | +.0 / -.0005 | -.0003 / -.0008 | -.0008 / -.0016 |
| .95 - 1.19 | +.0008 / +.0 | +.0023 / +.0018 | +.0013 / +.0008 | +.0003 / +.0002 | +.0 / -.0005 | -.0003 / -.0008 | -.0008 / -.0016 |
| 1.19 - 1.58 | +.001 / +.0 | +.0031 / +.0025 | +.0016 / +.001 | +.0004 / +.0002 | +.0 / -.0006 | -.0004 / -.001 | -.001 / -.002 |
| 1.58 - 1.97 | +.001 / +.0 | +.0034 / +.0028 | +.0016 / +.001 | +.0004 / +.0002 | +.0 / -.0006 | -.0004 / -.001 | -.001 / -.002 |
| 1.97 - 2.56 | +.0012 / +.0 | +.0042 / +.0035 | +.0021 / +.0014 | +.0004 / +.0003 | +.0 / -.0007 | -.0004 / -.0011 | -.0012 / -.0024 |
| 2.56 - 3.15 | +.0012 / +.0 | +.0047 / +.004 | +.0021 / +.0014 | +.0004 / +.0003 | +.0 / -.0007 | -.0004 / -.0011 | -.0012 / -.0024 |
| 3.15 - 3.94 | +.0014 / +.0 | +.0059 / +.005 | +.0025 / +.0016 | +.0005 / +.0004 | +.0 / -.0009 | -.0005 / -.0014 | -.0014 / -.0028 |
| 3.94 - 4.73 | +.0014 / +.0 | +.0069 / +.006 | +.0025 / +.0016 | +.0005 / +.0004 | +.0 / -.0009 | -.0005 / -.0014 | -.0014 / -.0028 |
| 4.73 - 5.52 | +.0016 / +.0 | +.008 / +.007 | +.0028 / +.0018 | +.0006 / +.0004 | +.0 / -.001 | -.0006 / -.0016 | -.0016 / -.0032 |
| 5.52 - 6.3 | +.0016 / +.0 | +.008 / +.007 | +.0028 / +.0018 | +.0006 / +.0004 | +.0 / -.001 | -.0006 / -.0016 | -.0016 / -.0032 |
| 6.3 - 7.09 | +.0016 / +.0 | +.009 / +.008 | +.0028 / +.0018 | +.0006 / +.0004 | +.0 / -.001 | -.0006 / -.0016 | -.0016 / -.0032 |

Fig.138. Table of Imperial Limits and Fits up to 7".

# TABLE OF METRIC LIMITS AND FITS UP TO 180mm.

| NOMINAL SIZES OVER - UP TO & INCLUDING | HOLES BASIC HOLE H7 | SHAFTS INTERFERENCE u6 SHRINK | p6 LIGHT PRESS | TRANS-ITION j6 PUSH | CLEARANCE h6 SLIDE | g6 CLOSE RUN | f7 RUN |
|---|---|---|---|---|---|---|---|
| 0 - 3 | +0.01 / +0 | +0.024 / +0.018 | +0.012 / +0.006 | +0.004 / - 0.002 | +0 / - 0.006 | -0.002 / -0.008 | -0.006 / -0.016 |
| 3 - 6 | +0.012 / +0 | +0.031 / +0.023 | +0.02 / +0.012 | +0.008 / - 0.002 | +0 / - 0.008 | -0.004 / -0.012 | -0.01 / -0.022 |
| 6 - 10 | +0.015 / +0 | +0.037 / +0.028 | +0.024 / +0.015 | +0.007 / - 0.002 | +0 / - 0.009 | -0.005 / -0.014 | -0.013 / -0.028 |
| 10 - 18 | +0.018 / +0 | +0.044 / +0.033 | +0.029 / +0.018 | +0.008 / - 0.003 | +0 / - 0.011 | -0.006 / -0.017 | -0.016 / -0.034 |
| 18 - 24 | +0.021 / +0 | +0.054 / +0.041 | +0.035 / +0.022 | +0.009 / - 0.004 | +0. / - 0.013 | -0.007 / -0.02 | -0.02 / -0.041 |
| 24 - 30 | | +0.061 / +0.048 | | | | | |
| 30 - 40 | +0.025 / +0 | +0.076 / +0.06 | +0.042 / +0.026 | +0.011 / - 0.005 | +0 / - 0.016 | -0.009 / -0.025 | -0.025 / -0.05 |
| 40 - 50 | | +0.086 / +0.07 | | | | | |
| 50 - 65 | +0.03 / +0 | +0.106 / +0.087 | +0.051 / +0.032 | +0.012 / - 0.007 | +0 / - 0.019 | -0.01 / -0.029 | -0.03 / -0.06 |
| 65 - 80 | | +0.121 / +0.102 | | | | | |
| 80 - 100 | +0.035 / +0 | +0.145 / +0.124 | +0.059 / +0.037 | +0.013 / - 0.009 | +0 / - 0.022 | -0.012 / -0.034 | -0.036 / -0.071 |
| 100 - 120 | | +0.166 / +0.144 | | | | | |
| 120 - 140 | +0.04 / +0 | +0.185 / +0.17 | +0.068 / +0.048 | +0.014 / - 0.011 | +0 / - 0.025 | -0.014 / -0.039 | -0.043 / -0.083 |
| 140 - 160 | | +0.215 / +0.19 | | | | | |
| 160 - 180 | | +0.235 / +0.21 | | | | | |

**Fig.139. Table of Metric Limits and Fits up to 180mm.**

**3**

| DIM. | FACTOR | DIM. | FACTOR |
|---|---|---|---|
| A | ·25000 | F | |
| B | ·43301 | G | |
| C | ·86603 | H | |
| D | | J | |
| E | | K | |

**5**

| DIM. | FACTOR | DIM. | FACTOR |
|---|---|---|---|
| A | ·40451 | F | |
| B | ·29389 | G | |
| C | ·58779 | H | |
| D | ·18164 | J | |
| E | ·55902 | K | |

**6**

| DIM. | FACTOR | DIM. | FACTOR |
|---|---|---|---|
| A | ·25000 | F | |
| B | ·43301 | G | |
| C | ·50000 | H | |
| D | | J | |
| E | | K | |

**7**

| DIM. | FACTOR | DIM. | FACTOR |
|---|---|---|---|
| A | ·33922 | F | ·39092 |
| B | ·21694 | G | |
| C | ·43388 | H | |
| D | ·27052 | J | |
| E | ·42300 | K | |

**8**

| DIM. | FACTOR | DIM. | FACTOR |
|---|---|---|---|
| A | ·14645 | F | |
| B | ·14645 | G | |
| C | ·35355 | H | |
| D | ·35355 | J | |
| E | | K | |

**9**

| DIM. | FACTOR | DIM. | FACTOR |
|---|---|---|---|
| A | ·21985 | F | ·32139 |
| B | ·26200 | G | ·17101 |
| C | ·34302 | H | ·33682 |
| D | ·63302 | J | |
| E | ·27060 | K | |

**10**

| DIM. | FACTOR | DIM. | FACTOR |
|---|---|---|---|
| A | ·25000 | F | |
| B | ·29389 | G | |
| C | ·18164 | H | |
| D | ·30902 | J | |
| E | ·09549 | K | |

**11**

| DIM. | FACTOR | DIM. | FACTOR |
|---|---|---|---|
| A | ·47975 | F | ·25627 |
| B | ·14087 | G | ·42063 |
| C | ·23701 | H | ·27032 |
| D | ·15232 | J | ·18450 |
| E | ·11704 | K | ·21292 |

**12**

| DIM. | FACTOR | DIM. | FACTOR |
|---|---|---|---|
| A | ·06699 | FF | ·25000 |
| B | ·43301 | GG | |
| C | ·25000 | HH | |
| D | ·43301 | JJ | |
| E | ·06699 | KK | |

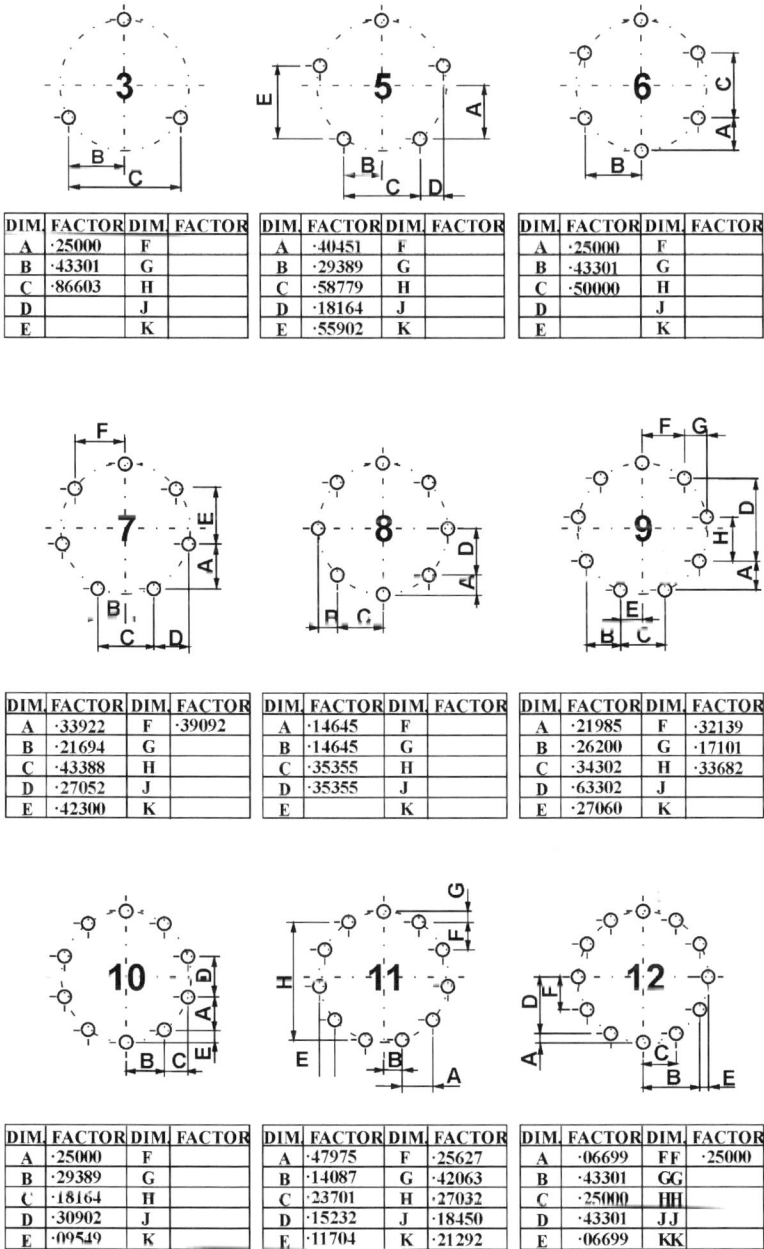

Fig.140. Co-ordinates for Holes on P. C. D.

135

# LIST OF ILLUSTRATIONS.

1. A typical internet technical drawing.

2. Collar with a blind keyway.

3. Collar with a through keyway.

4. "The Biscuit Tin".

5. "The Biscuit Tin" mounted on the Boring Table.

6. The situation when machining the inner pads.

7. "The Biscuit Tin" with viewing slots.

8. Choosing the Datums.

9. Transferring a Datum to a hole.

10. Bad and Good Arrowheads.

11. Typical CAD and Pencil drawings.

12. Pencil sharpened with a pencil sharpener.

13. Small craft knife.

14. First Stage in sharpening a drawing pencil.

15. Second Stage in sharpening a drawing pencil.

16. Clutch and Propelling drawing pencils.

17. Various Lines and their Usages.

18. Bad and Good Ways of Vertical Dimensioning.

19. Simple Block with basic dimensions.

20. First Angle Projection.

21. Third Angle Projection.

22. Two Ways of Stating Third Angle Projection.

23. Isometric Projection and Third Angle Projection.

24. Tolerance Methods.

25. Graph of Cost v Tolerance.

26. Projecting lines.

27. Table of common abbreviations.

28. Double Dimensioning.

29. Dimensional flow.

30. Solving the problem.

31. Dimensioning an Angle.

32. Dimensioning a Centre Line.

33. Crossing Dimension Lines.

34. Crossed and Open Dimension Lines.

35. Dimensioning a hatched section.

36. Direct and Indirect Dimension Figures.

37. Combined measuring systems.

38. Plan of Plate with 4 blocks.

39. Section on 'AA' of Plate with 4 blocks.

40. Corrected Section on 'AA' of Plate with 4 blocks.

41. Dimensioning a fairly thin part.

42. Dimensioning a very thin part.

43. Dimensioning a laminate assembly.

44. Dimensioning a radius.

45. Two blocks to be fastened to a plate.

46. Dimensioning sets of linked holes.

47. Dimensioning an assembly.

48. Cumulative Dimensioning.

49. Pitch Circle Diameter.

50. Non-Cumulative Dimensioning.

51. Development in the method of showing screw threads.

52. The Reminder Notice.

53. Small plate.

54. Small plate, Best Case Scenario.

55. Small plate, Worst Case Scenario.

56. Block with one hole.

57. Block with two holes.

58. Block with three holes.

59. Cast Iron Plate.

60. Drilled Strip.

61. Ventilation Duct Flange.

62. Duct Flange Blanking Plate.

63. Small Plate working from Datum.

64. Small Plate working from Reference dimension.

65. Pipe Flange.

66. Block with two holes.

67. Block with three holes.

68. Cast Iron Plate.

69. Drilled Strip.

70. Ventilation Duct Flange.

71. Duct Flange Blanking Plate.

72. Small Plate working from Datum.

73. Small Plate working from Reference dimension.

74. Pipe Flange.

75. Piston.

76. L.N.E.R. Anti-Vacuum Valve.

77. Horizontal Stuffing Box.

78. Stepped Shaft.

79. 'V' Block.

80. Eccentric Sheave and Strap.

81. Machine Shaft (80A Left Hand; 80B Right Hand).

82. Tabular Format for Holes.

83. Tabular Format for Shafts.

84. Shrink Fit.

85. Press Fit.

86. Push Fit.

87. Slide Fit.

88. Running Fit.

89. Extract from Imperial Table.

90. Abridged extract from Imperial Table.

91. Dowel Symbol.

92. Typical analysis of the parts of a Mechanism.

93. Item List for the Mechanism Parts Analysis.

94. Water Tap, or Faucet, with parts marked.

95. Item List for Water Tap, or Faucet.


## 'C' SERIES EXERCISE ANSWERS.

96. Block with one hole, Worst Case Scenario.

97. Block with two holes, Worst Case Scenario.

98. Block with three holes, Worst Case Scenario.

99. Cast Iron Plate, Worst Case Scenario.

100. Cast Iron Plate, new design.

101. Drilled Strip, Worst Case Scenario.

102. Ventilation Duct Flange, Worst Case Scenario.

103. Duct Flange Blanking Plate, Worst Case Scenario.

104. Duct Flange and Flange Plate.

105. Small Plate working from Datum.

106. Small Plate working from Reference dimension.

107. Pipe Flange, Worst Case Scenario.


## 'N' SERIES EXERCISE ANSWERS.

108. Block with two holes.

109. Block with three holes.

110. Cast Iron Plate.

111. Drilled Strip.

112. Ventilation Duct Flange.

113. Duct Flange Blanking Plate.

114. The Duct Flange and Blanking Plate.

115. Small Plate working from Datum.

116. Small Plate working from Reference dimension.

117. Pipe Flange


## 'P' SERIES EXERCISE ANSWERS.

118. Piston.

119. L.N.E.R. Anti-Vacuum Valve.

120. Horizontal Stuffing Box.

121. Stepped Shaft.

122. 'V' Block.

123. Eccentric Sheave and Strap.

124. Machine Shaft.

## PRESENTATIONS REWORKED

125. Piston (revised).

126. L.N.E.R. Anti-Vacuum Valve (revised).

127. Horizontal Stuffing Box (revised).

128. Stepped Shaft (revised).

129. 'V' Block (revised).

130. Eccentric Sheave and Strap (revised).

131. Machine Shaft (revised).

## THE DONKEY SYNDROME

132. Set of Tiles.

133. Tiles with Mating Faces Shown as Datums.

134. Tile Dimensions.

135. Tile with the Donkey Dimension.

136. Tile with Minimal Dimensions.

137. Tile with All Axial Dimensions

Figs.1, 11, 75 to 83, 89, 90, 118 to 124, 138 and 139 redrawn from original text by the author.
Remainder of drawings by the author.
Figs. 13 and 16 photographs by the author.
Cover design by the author.

All drawings were computer-aided, but with an arts package and not CAD.

In association with Southport College Engineering Department.

# ABOUT THE AUTHOR

Geoff was educated at Liverpool Collegiate School, before serving an apprenticeship as a Toolmaker with D. Napier & Sons Ltd.. and then became a Design Draughtsman. Meanwhile he gained his Post National Certificate and became a Graduate of the Institution of Production Engineers. He was a computer programmer in 1964, working on second-generation mainframes.

After National Service in the RAF as an Education Instructor he began his career as an Industrial Designer, becoming a Chartered Engineer and a Member of the Institution of Production Engineers in 1968. He has been a senior manager in design and development for many years and his last position was that of Industrial Engineering Manager for a technical ceramics company.

He has a wide range of interests and hobbies of which model making is only one. Even there his range is wide, covering many different types of model, both engineering and architectural. He was a computer programmer in 1964 on a Second Generation Mainframe, and having studied six languages he has been an Egyptologist for 40 years and can read Egyptian hieroglyphs.

He has lectured at Riverside College's engineering workshop technology classes and now does so at Southport College.

19071023R00081

Printed in Great Britain
by Amazon